I0558832

COPYRIGHT
Copyright © 2025 by Zachary Italian

PUBLISHER
You Deserve More Media

First You Deserve More Media edition April 2024
Second You Deserve More Media edition September 2024

You Deserve More is a registered trademark of Publishing House LLC

For information about special discounts for bulk purchases, please contact You Deserve More Media sales at team@youdeservemoremedia.com

The You Deserve More Media Speakers Bureau can bring authors to your live events.
For more information, or to book an event, visit our website at www.youdeservemore.media

Interior design by Zachary Italian
Manufactured in the United States of America

Library of Congress Cataloging-in-Publication Data has been applied for.

ISBN: 979-8-9903411-1-1

DISCLAIMER

1

Dedication

To my sister, Skyler, and my brother, Jaden, for the shared experiences that have shaped us.

To my wife, for her unending love and support in every step of our journey.

To my parents, for their wisdom and the foundations they built.

And to all the future Italians who follow in our footsteps, carrying our heritage and dreams into tomorrow.

The Company of You

Chart the Course of Your Destiny and Become the Architect of Your Success

Zachary Italian

Publishing House
PHILADELPHIA | NEW YORK | NEWARK

2nd Edition

3

Contents

Preface

Welcome to "The Company of You." This is not just a book - it's a testament to the entrepreneurial spirit. A narrative that resonates with anyone who has ever dared to dream and then turned that dream into reality.

My journey, much like yours, has been about creating and climbing my own ladder. It started with vision – a vision to make a difference, not just in my life but in the lives of those I could reach. From building and growing Village Helpdesk to teaching and empowering others as an educator, my path has always been about innovation, education, and perseverance. Through trial and tribulation, I have learned that the true essence of success lives in the relentless pursuit of our passions. This book is my attempt to encapsulate that essence. It's about viewing our lives as the ultimate enterprise, where we are the founders, the strategists, and the driving forces behind our WHY.

Here, we will explore some theories that have guided my journey – principles that can help anyone become the CEO of their life. From developing strategic partnerships to enhancing customer experiences and managing diverse projects, the lessons here are drawn from real-life experiences and challenges. This book is a guide for those who aspire to take control of their destiny, to invest in themselves, and to build their own ladders to success.

Introduction

As you embark on the pages that follow this introduction, please know that I am truly grateful for the privilege to have you reading this. What I hope to deliver is a journey that travels further than the boundaries of conventional thought theory and personal growth. This journey is about realizing the potential of the most influential entity in your life – You.

In "The Company of You," you are the central character. This book speaks to transforming every aspect of your life into a thriving, well-oiled enterprise. It's about adopting the mindset of a CEO in your life – strategizing, making decisions, and leading with purpose and vision.

We will delve into the dynamics of personal branding, exploring how to harness your unique skills, experiences, and passions. You'll learn to apply the same principles that drive successful businesses to your personal goals and aspirations.

Strategic planning, to skill development. From overcoming obstacles, to seizing opportunities. Each chapter is a steppingstone towards your personal and professional fulfillment. Whether you are looking to reinvent your career, enhance your personal relationships, or simply find more meaning in your daily life; you'll find valuable insights and tools here.

This is not just about reading a book, this is about writing your own story. The story of someone who took the reins of their life with confidence and vision and steered it toward a horizon of their own making.

Welcome to the Company of You – it's time to take your seat at the head of the boardroom table of your life.

1

Welcome to the Company of You

It is your first day as the CEO of the most important company in the world. We are all relying on you to steer this ship into success. Even though there is a lot on your plate - we are all counting on you to know when we should jump, and how high.

The Company of You is an organization unlike any other. It has unique strengths, challenges, and opportunities, just like yourself.

As the CEO you will need to develop strategies on how to leverage these strengths, overcome said challenges, and seize mentioned opportunities. In these pages you will read through the ideas of how best to go about this. These steps are meant to help you uncover your unique potential and think outside the box.

Not everything you read here is it to be literally taken. Many of the ideas in this book are meant to encourage a new way of thinking into your mind or introduce a new idea completely. Thought crafting, if you will.

Along the way, I will provide you with practical tools, strategies, and thoughts that I have had along my journey.

Change can be daunting. Just remember, the faster you learn to fail the faster you will learn to succeed.

It is your job is to discover and know your unique self. First and foremost, we are all uniquely us, and this is where our super-powers live. One of the most crucial facts you need to understand to be a successful leader is that YOU are special. You need to understand that the world needs your unique perspective and contributions. Kindling the flame of passion within ourselves is crucial, so first thing first is for you to learn to recognize the gems that make you uniquely you. You need to actively embrace yourself because in this world you cannot rely on anyone else to do it for you. It will be important for you to understand that there is a lifelong learner within you that has no limitations. You think, therefore you are.

You are limitless, and for everything you are not, you are.

Our goal here is to dig deep into your interests and desires for the fuel that will propel you forward on your path to self-actualization.

Strategic planning is our compass. Strategy is what we are trying to build upon. The power of vision is at the center of our strategic planning.

Just as successful corporations are committed to their employee's continuous learning and development, we, as individuals, must also dedicate ourselves to unending personal growth. Throughout this text we repeat the importance in exploring strategies that promote self-improvement. This is to ensure that you are constantly challenged to develop and skillfully manage the intricacies of life's challenges.

Your journey into personal growth truly begins with the recognition that we are all perpetual students. Our aim is to not only encourage this grueling type of self-improvement but also for you to create an affinity and yearning for the experience.

Understand that investing in yourself is not only an act of self-care but also a strategic move towards success.

The world is in a constant state of flux, and adaptation is key to survival. It is important for you to learn to embrace change and chaos. Just as organizations adapt to changing market conditions, we must learn to embrace change in our own lives.

Embracing change can open new doors and lead to personal breakthroughs. Flexibility is key to maintaining alignment with your life's course.

Another key skill to survival and success is resilience.

Resilience serves as a critical defense mechanism, safeguarding individuals from the inevitable setbacks and adversities encountered in life.

By examining the components that contribute to resilience, such as emotional intelligence, adaptability, and stress management, we can discover how to rebound from adversity and keep a positive outlook.

A growth mindset is the cornerstone of personal development. In the final section, we will emphasize the importance of nurturing this growth mindset.

Understand that your abilities and intelligence are not fixed but can be developed through dedication and hard work. Embrace challenges as opportunities for growth and let your growth mindset propel you toward self-identification and personal excellence.

As you settle into your role as CEO, and a lifelong learner, you will begin to harness the power of self-actualization. The power of understanding who you truly are.

You will begin to positively adapt to change, naturally practice resilience, and find yourself sprinting towards uncomfortable situations. These are the first building blocks to your skeleton key that unlocks the doors to your full potential.

Remember that your ongoing evolution is a testament to the commitment you're making to yourself. This is the start of a journey towards becoming the best version of you.

The strategy you come up with will serve as your guiding star on the forever journey to self-identification. As you harness the power of vision, define your life's mission, set goals, craft strategic plans, and embrace adaptation, you become and remain the architect of your life's course. Strategic planning is not a rigid template but a dynamic framework that evolves with you.

The Power of Vision comes next. The essence of strategic planning is rooted in the potency of vision. This chapter initiates our exploration into the criticality of visualizing your future aspirations. Speaking of vision, we break this down into an equation that allows you to put numbers to thoughts for actionable insights into your overall vision of you and your brand.

Vision is something we should have inherently, but without proper training and realization people's vision often become disillusioned and more of a dystopian dream than a realistic opportunity. Your actions guide your vision both subconsciously and consciously.

Just as organizations define their missions, our vision is the viewpoint of our bigger quest line. Explore the significance of understanding your purpose and values. Your mission statement will become the foundation upon which you build a life that aligns with your deepest aspirations. You will learn how to transform your dreams into actionable, well-defined objectives. Understand that setting goals that empower you and allow you to track your progress are very important to our mission.

It is also important for you to understand the true meaning of assets. Assets are not just things on your balance sheet. Assets are also relationships, experiences, and specialized knowledge. Learn to appreciate, acknowledge, and identify, your unique talents, skills, and relationships as assets in your journey toward self-identification. We will speak on this more to understand that assets are not just financial resources but also your intellectual, emotional, and social capital.

Finally, we will continue to harp on ongoing improvement as the driving force behind progress. You will learn my philosophy of continuous improvement, examining how small, incremental changes can lead to significant advancements in your life.

Explore methods such as Kaizen and agile thinking to adapt, evolve, and refine your strategies as you journey toward self-identification. Just as quality assurance ensures the reliability of products and services, integrating quality assurance into your life guarantees that your actions and decisions align with your values and objectives. We will discuss the importance of setting and maintaining high standards in various aspects of your life, from relationships to personal projects. Embrace a commitment to quality to achieve excellence in all that you do.

In contrary to the idea of being extreme is what it takes to succeed; Balance is the key to sustained success. In this book, we also explore the art of balance and its significance in your daily operations. You will need to learn to juggle the various aspects of your life in The Company of You, including work: personal growth, relationships, and leisure. The goal here is to achieve equilibrium and prevent burnout by introducing self-care and time management techniques.

Now that we have begun to peel back the layers of our own complexity, uncovering the multifaceted nature of our personal enterprise, let us now turn our gaze inward, to a landscape rich with hidden talents and strengths. With the map of self-awareness in hand, let us venture deeper into the heart of our individuality. Remember, the journey of self-improvement is ever-unfolding, and each step forward is a step toward the realization of our most authentic selves.

So, as we transition from the introduction of our story to the heart of the matter, let us do so with the courage and conviction that the journey ahead is one of significance.

Onward to Chapter 2, where the real adventure begins, and where we will learn to identify, appreciate, and elevate our strengths and talents, setting the stage for a future bound for achievement and fulfillment.

2

Understanding The Difference

In psychology, exist two concepts of us.

There are the "I" and the "me," which are the two overarching categories of our self and identity. While these terms are sometimes used interchangeably in everyday language, they possess distinct meanings in the field of psychology.

"I" is associated with the concept of the self as a subjective, conscious, and active agent.

It refers to the part of an individual's identity that experiences thoughts, emotions, and actions. The "I" is the aspect of the self that is actively engaged in decision-making, self-reflection, and self-awareness. In the context of the self, the "I" can be thought of as the experiencer or the knower.

"Me," on the other hand, is associated with the concept of the self as an object of one's own awareness.

It represents the various roles, attributes, and aspects of an individual's identity that can be observed or described.

The "me" includes an individual's self-concept, self-esteem, and social identity. In this context, the "me" can be thought of as the known or the experienced.

These concepts were introduced by American psychologist

George Herbert Mead in his work on social psychology and symbolic interactionism. According to Mead, the "I" and the "me" are both essential components of the self, emerging through social interactions and internal reflections.

The "I" represents the spontaneous, impulsive, and creative aspect of the self, while the "me" embodies the learned, socialized, and reflective aspect of the self. To summarize, the "I" and the "me" are distinct yet interconnected aspects of the self in psychology. The "I" refers to the subjective, conscious, and active agent, while the "me" represents the objective, observable, and social aspects of one's identity.

It is important to understand to difference of these because we are often limited by the beliefs of others, and even more often petrified into believing we are who others say we are.

Well, we are not what others think… We are what our actions prove us to be.

You are only limited by what you believe your limits are. This mindset is necessary when trying to evaluate your own abilities. The goal is to make unbiased decisions about yourself and your ability.

By honestly evaluating your abilities - you can honestly identify your strengths and understand where you excel, and where more training is needed. To initiate the process of analyzing your skillset, start by assessing your current skills.

This encompasses both hard skills, such as technical competencies and specialized knowledge, as well as soft skills like communication, problem-solving, and people management. Both skillsets are important, but in the world of technology, and AI, soft skills are something you may want to put extra focus into.

Take the time to create a list of your skills and abilities, along with relevant achievements, experiences, and qualifications. For this comprehension, focus on the "I."

Here's a table template to assist you in compiling your skills, abilities, achievements, experiences, and qualifications:

Category	Skill/Ability	Experience	Qualification
Hard Skill	Program in Python	Developed a web app using Flask	Python Programming Certificate
Soft Skill	Public Speaking	Presented at a conference	Participating Member of Toastmasters
Soft Skill	Team Collaboration	Orchestrated a cross-departmental team for a product launch.	Team Leadership Workshop

Feel free to add or remove rows as needed to accommodate all your skills, abilities, accomplishments, experiences, and qualifications.

This table will help you take inventory and visualize your specific soft skills, specific hard skills, and strengths.

Once you have a clear understanding of your current skills, it's time to pinpoint your areas of expertise. Based on your assessment, identify where you excel and the areas where you stand out. Do you have any soft skills or hard skills you do not often find in others you come across? Were there any skills you listed that you felt very strongly about while writing? From your list, we want to understand the uniqueness of what you have to offer.

This will help you to leverage your strengths and use them to your advantage. For example, if you excel at public speaking, you can use this skill to become a thought leader in your industry or community. If this is the case, I may have opportunities for you to stand up and speak about the Company of You!

However, it's also important to recognize where you need to improve. Pinpointing areas for growth will allow you to develop a personal growth plan that enables you to continue to develop your skills and abilities efficiently. This could include taking courses, attending workshops, or seeking mentorship from your community, which we will deep dive later. As humans it is increasingly more important to be well-rounded.

Ultimately, the chief aim is to have the data available to successfully develop a plan for achieving your desired skill set. What we will speak on later is how to identify the specific skills you wish to cultivate, analyze the resources available for learning, and a create a timeline to reach your objectives.

We accomplish this by dividing your goals into short-term and long-term targets and devise actionable steps to attain them. It is best to view large goals as projects that contain many various smaller sub-sets of tasks and goals to accomplish. This is a more realistic vision and approach for any type of goal-accomplishing activity.

For instance, if you aim to enhance your marketing skills, you might begin by enrolling in a marketing course or participating in a marketing conference – not pitching the most successful person you know on a marketing campaign you do not have the insight to pull-off.

Additionally, you can also subscribe to pertinent marketing blogs and magazines, join marketing networks or communities, and even volunteer for marketing roles within non-profit organizations or startups.

Please note I am not telling you to not make pitches and seize opportunities you are confident in, but for most situations there are many smaller actionable steps or goals that can be reached that would make for the larger aspirations to even become a real opportunity. It is incredibly easy to overestimate what can be accomplished in a year, and it is even easier to underestimate what can be accomplished in ten.

Creative and analytical proficiencies are. both vital, so remember to stay human when studying the technical or else you will get wrapped up into the mathematician mindset and lose connection to the soft skills that we are longing for in this era.

Now let's apply the same idea to a different topic of study. Let's say you are planning to learn more about technology. Here are some activates you can partake in when trying to learn more about technology:

Consider enrolling in technology-focused courses or obtaining certifications aligned with your goals, such as coding boot camps, data science courses, or AWS certifications.

Engage in tech forums and communities, attending industry conferences, and subscribing to tech-oriented media sources will help you stay current with the latest trends and insights.

Do not overlook the practical dimension.

Stay involved with personal projects or spend time assisting with open-source initiatives. Putting action with valuable experience will create tangible work samples you may include in your portfolio. Do not overlook participating hackathons or coding competitions. By staying active in the industry's community will strengthen your technical skills while offering opportunities for collaboration and networking.

Starting at the ground level in your field is like getting a front-row seat to the action—it's where the learning happens in real time. Even though you are the boss, try to stay involved in every level as an you can as an equal and peer. Think of it this way: every entry-level job is a chance to get your hands dirty with the very skills you're eager to master. These basic skills are the foundations to which your bigger aspirations are built from.

For me, the journey began with reaching out to people who found themselves where I wanted to be. I learned by doing, right alongside them, and those entry-level roles quickly became launchpads for growth because I was actively learning from those around me, and leading me.

It's about diving in, asking questions, and not being afraid to tackle the tasks at hand. Think of each day as a new opportunity to build upon what you know, to make mistakes and learn from them. It's in these roles that you'll find mentors and friends who will show you the ropes, share their own experiences, and help you navigate your path forward.

Your journey of skill enhancement is much like adding tools to your toolkit. Every new task, every problem solved, adds another tool, another skill. And as you move from one role to another, your toolkit grows, making you more adept and versatile on the field.

Remember, the goal isn't just to collect skills, but to weave them into the fabric of your identity.

It's about understanding that learning never stops.
The more you grow, the more you'll find areas you want to explore and improve upon. And that's a good thing! It means you're pushing yourself, not settling for what you already know.

In this pursuit of continuous growth, remember to periodically take stock of your skills.

What have you learned?

What do you want to learn next?

Adjusting your goals and strategies is part of the journey. It ensures that you're always moving forward, always aiming for the next milestone in the Company of You.

Analyzing your skillset is an ongoing process. As you continue to evolve and grow, allocate time to reassess and adapt your goals and strategies accordingly. Remember, we are but perpetual students.

Embracing your uniqueness in a world that often champions conformity is a feat easier said than done. The power of individuality can often be daunting. However, it is our distinct qualities that ultimately mold our experiences, shape our accomplishments, and determine the value we contribute to the world – so owning our individuality is crucial to building the life experiences we long for.

Acknowledging, celebrating, and harnessing what sets us apart is pivotal to charting our own paths and aligning with opportunities that genuinely resonate with us.

It is important to not only recognize the attributes that differentiate us from others, but also embrace them. Embracing your uniqueness will embolden you to carve your own niche, showcase your talents, and attract opportunities that harmonize with your authentic self.

Drawing from my own experiences, I've come to realize that we all have only one true thing in common— and that is our uniqueness.

We are all so remarkably different. We are almost as different as we are similar.

Embracing your distinctiveness is a fundamental facet of personal branding and self-actualization. By acknowledging and celebrating these attributes that set you apart, you equip yourself to stand out and magnetize opportunities that align with your genuine self. This journey towards authenticity and personal differentiation is not about seeking attention for its sake, but about giving attention your identity and offering your unique perspective to the world.

Take another moment to again engage in introspection and explore what sets you apart and makes you extraordinary. This time let's focus more on the emotional context of yourself. Not your skills, like how fast you can solve quantum algorithms or how well you are able put together a spreadsheet. Think of things like your personable traits, and your unique life experiences.

We are shifting our focus back towards the pragmatic "I."

This "I" is the part of you engaged in decision-making, self-reflection, and objective self-awareness. To approach this idea in the perspective of "I" while analyzing your skill set in the ideology of "Me" enables you to objectively evaluate your attributes, strengths, and areas for improvement.

Embracing your uniqueness involves taking pride in your identity and boldly showcasing your authentic self. This can include sharing your talents and experiences with others, and confidently voicing your opinions and ideas.

It's crucial to grasp that embracing your uniqueness doesn't involve attempting to fit into a predefined mold or conforming to societal expectations. Instead, it means fully embracing you, and the company of you.

Remember, the only true commonality among humans is our inherent diversity. Embracing your uniqueness not only empowers you but also allows you to connect with individuals who recognize, appreciate, and respect your' 'you'... Therefore, celebrate what sets you apart and leverage it to shape a life and personal brand that authentically represents who you are.

People do not care about how much you know, until
they know about how much you care."
– Theodore Roosevelt

Let's delve into passions. The path to self-awareness
requires discovering what truly excites you—those
activities, interests, or concepts that light up your soul and
bring you happiness and contentment. Immersing yourself
in passions can lead to your flow state, a magical
timelessness where everything else fades away, leaving you
deeply connected with what you love doing.

To realize your passions, begin by reflecting on the
activities that bring you the greatest joy and fulfillment.
They could be hobbies, interests, or even just past
experiences that deeply resonated with you.

When these passions are nurtured, they can flourish and
expand, influencing various facets of your life. They not
only provide personal enjoyment but also offer avenues to
enhance your skills, broaden your knowledge, and
potentially chart a career path that aligns with your genuine
loves.

The aim is to actively integrate passions our daily routine,
seek out like-minded individuals, and explore opportunities
to develop and learn within your areas of interest.

Our passions are not meant to be solitary entities; rather, they are best when intertwined with our daily activities, work, and interactions with others.

This is where the philosophies of Aristotle, Jean-Paul Sartre, the Stoics, Confucius, and Buddhist teachings find common ground.

These philosophers all emphasized the significance of harmonizing one's passions and interests with their daily activities and work, underscoring that a fulfilling life entails a balance between what we do and what we love.

One of the most pivotal aspects of personal growth and success involves exploring and embracing your passions. Engaging in activities and pursuits that bring you joy, fulfillment, and a sense of purpose give you the keys to unlock your wellspring of untapped potential.

First, we start by identifying the activities and pursuits that bring you the utmost joy and fulfillment. You will know these activities if you think of what you are doing when time escapes you.

When you are carrying out these tasks or activities you completely lose yourself in the time and obsess over the finer details. You think about the possibilities and outcomes, you are competitive. This activity, this action, this maybe a passion of yours.

To further your journey, actively identify the talents and strengths utilized in your passions, reflecting on how these align with your personal values and beliefs. Dedicate a moment to contemplate, what about the activities bring you joy and fulfillment?

Consider which pursuits allow you to lose track of time,

immersing you in a state of flow where your talents and passions unite seamlessly. Identifying these key passions is essential for aligning your personal desires with your professional objectives. Treat passions as seeds requiring nurturing to fully blossom.

Make it a habit to allocate specific times for diving into activities that ignite your passions. Build a network of like-minded individuals who echo your enthusiasm. Actively seek out avenues to polish your skills and expand your knowledge in areas you're deeply passionate about.

Incorporating your passions into "The Company of You" isn't just motivational speak - it's a strategic business decision that propels growth. Think of your passions as your startup's unique value proposition—they set you apart and drive you toward notable achievements that are only revealed to the eye of the believer. Let these interests be your north star, guiding your decisions and helping you navigate challenges. By integrating what you love into your daily operations, you're not just enhancing your own path but you're also setting a standard and inspiring those around you. This approach is what creates a thriving enterprise, where passion meets purpose.

Throughout history, great philosophers have deeply pondered what makes life truly fulfilling. Time and again, they've highlighted a crucial insight: the key to a meaningful existence lies in aligning our passions and interests with our daily actions and work. This principle of living a life in harmony with what we love is a powerful theme woven into the fabric of many philosophical teachings, underlining its universal importance across cultures and epochs.

From earlier reference, Aristotle, in his concept of eudaimonia, or flourishing, insists that a life of value is one where an individual engages in activities congruent with their virtues and inherent talents. By integrating one's passions into life and work, an individual can cultivate a profound sense of purpose and fulfillment.

Adding to that, it's not just Aristotle who was onto something. The stoic philosophers, including the likes of Epictetus and Marcus Aurelius, also acknowledged the significance of aligning one's actions with their values and inner compass. They held that when we act in harmony with our genuine nature and pursue our passions, we become more resilient and better equipped to confront life's challenges. The Stoics believed finding peace and contentment was all about making sure our inner world and our actions were in sync, highlighting how staying true to ourselves in our daily lives really matters. This shared wisdom from different corners of the world tells us loud and clear: living a life rich in purpose and fulfillment comes from embracing and acting on our passions.

Similarly, Jean-Paul Sartre, the existentialist philosopher, emphasized the importance of living authentically and staying true to oneself. He argued that by courageously embracing our freedom and pursuing what genuinely aligns with our values, we can uncover deeper meaning in our lives. Sartre believed that transcending the constraints of societal norms allows us to live more fully, crafting a life that reflects our true essence.

In the Eastern tradition, Confucius taught that a fulfilling life is achieved through cultivating virtues and nurturing one's unique talents. He emphasized that by bringing passion into our work and daily activities, we can create a sense of inner harmony that resonates with the world around us. Confucius saw personal growth as inseparable from the collective well-being of society, suggesting that when we align our passions and talents with our roles in the community, we not only grow as individuals but also contribute to the greater harmony and understanding within the fabric of our shared lives.

This perspective highlights a profound connection: when we pursue our true passions and refine our unique talents, we not only find personal fulfillment but also strengthen the bonds that hold society together. Confucius's wisdom elegantly bridges the pursuit of individual authenticity with the well-being of the community, showing us that our personal growth can serve as a cornerstone for collective harmony and prosperity.

The value of integrating passions into one's life and work is also reflected in the Buddhist concept of the "Middle Way." This philosophy advocates for balance and moderation in all aspects of life, including the pursuit of personal interests and the cultivation of meaningful endeavors. These teachings highlight that a fulfilling life is achieved through the seamless integration of passions into everyday activities and professional pursuits. Whether by embracing new hobbies, infusing enthusiasm into current projects, or exploring uncharted career paths, individuals can discover purpose and authenticity. Such a life is characterized by resilience, balance, and a deep connection to one's true self.

The process of integrating your passions into your life and work starts with profound introspection on your true interests, values, and sources of joy and fulfillment.

Once you have a clear comprehension of your passions you can start to analyze your current situation and identify areas where you can incorporate these passions. To carve out space for your passions in your daily routine, you might decide to dedicate time to hobbies or activities that relate with your interests. This could mean joining clubs, attending workshops, or taking part in community events where you can connect with others who share your enthusiasm.

When it pertains to your professional life, consider avenues through which you can infuse your passions into your existing role. This could be proposing innovative projects, collaborating with colleagues who resonate with your interests, or volunteering for additional responsibilities that align with your passions.

If you're feeling stuck in your current job, lacking the spark of passion that makes work feel meaningful, it might be time to look beyond the confines of your 9-to-5 for fulfillment. Think of this as an opportunity to embark on an adventure. Starting a side project or a small business that's close to your heart isn't just about doing what you love. It's about rediscovering yourself and what makes you tick.

Imagine crafting a space where your passions not only live but thrive. This endeavor isn't just a hobby... it's a garden where your creativity and skills grow, blossom, and possibly even bear financial fruits. It's about creating a life where work doesn't feel like work because it's intertwined with what you genuinely love. And who knows? This journey might lead you to unexpected destinations, opening doors to new pathways and opportunities that align with your deepest aspirations.

Connecting with like-minded individuals who share your passions can be a transformative step toward weaving what you love into every aspect of your life and career. Attending conferences, joining professional groups, or engaging in online discussions not only broadens your network but also introduces you to fresh perspectives and fosters a sense of belonging. These connections often spark meaningful relationships, insightful exchanges, and a supportive community that fuels your growth and ambitions.

At the same time, it's essential to prioritize self-care and cultivate a healthy balance between work and life. Infusing your passions into your daily activities and career should bring joy and enhance your overall well-being, not overwhelm you. Stay curious, embrace lifelong learning, and continuously explore the interests that inspire you. Your passions are uniquely yours, a vital part of your identity. By fully embracing them, you can unlock new opportunities, discover hidden talents, and create a life that is deeply fulfilling and purposeful, both for yourself and for the community you help to shape.

As you embark on the journey of exploring your passions within the Company of You, keep in mind that these passions play a pivotal role in your personal and professional evolution. Embrace the joy, fulfillment, and sense of purpose that emerge from aligning your strengths with your passions. Nurture these passions with intent and care, allowing them to propel your voyage of self-discovery and achievement. The Company of You eagerly anticipates the distinct contributions and remarkable accomplishments that will unfold as you embrace and unleash the potency of your passions. Let your passions act as the guiding beacon propelling you toward success.

Training & Development

Infinite Learning

Within The Company of You, we understand the profound importance of continuous improvement and lifelong learning. This chapter dives deep into the realm of training and development, inviting you to embrace a mindset of infinite learning. By committing to this journey, you open doors to endless possibilities, empowering yourself to reach new heights of personal and professional growth.

As you journey forward, keep in mind the wisdom of Jim Rohn, who said, "Your personal growth is not only for you. It's for all the people who will benefit from the person you become." Your commitment to developing your talents not only reshapes your life but also propels the success of The Company of You. By nurturing your abilities, you're not just elevating yourself. You're also enhancing the lives of those around you, spreading inspiration, knowledge, and positive change within your circle and beyond.

Just as a successful company invests in developing its employees' skills, you must prioritize nurturing your own abilities to unlock your full potential and achieve extraordinary success.

In The Company of You your growth and development are at the heart of everything we do. We understand that continuous improvement is essential for your journey towards self-actualization.

So, let's explore some key strategies and techniques that will empower you to cultivate your abilities and thrive in every aspect of your life:

The Company of You is committed to fostering an environment that encourages continuous improvement. We believe that learning is not confined to a single event or a static set of skills. Instead, it is an ongoing process that unfolds throughout your life.

In this chapter, we explore various avenues for growth and development, from formal training programs and educational resources to mentorship and experiential learning. By embracing growth opportunities, you position yourself at the forefront of personal and professional excellence.

First, let's understanding a few important concepts to keep in mind while reading…

Perpetual Student Mindset: Embrace the mindset of continuous learning, where curiosity and a thirst for knowledge propel you forward. Seek out opportunities for growth through formal education, online courses, workshops, and seminars. Be open to new ideas and diverse perspectives, constantly expanding your horizons. Remember, learning is not confined to classrooms—it happens everywhere and at all stages of life.

Train for Skill Mastery: Identify the skills that are crucial for your personal and professional goals and develop a deliberate plan to enhance these skills through practice, focused study, and hands-on experiences. Embrace challenges that push your boundaries and allow you to sharpen your abilities. Remember, skill mastery is a journey, and consistent effort and dedication are the keys to achieving excellence.

Encourage Collaborative Connections: Surround yourself with a network of supportive individuals who share your drive for growth and success. Collaborate with like-minded peers, engage in meaningful conversations, and learn from each other's experiences. Seek out mentors and coaches who can guide you on your path, providing valuable insights and wisdom. Together, we can achieve more and support one another's journey of development.

Ask for Feedback and Reflection: Embrace feedback as a catalyst for growth within The Company of You Seek input from trusted mentors, colleagues, and loved ones to gain different perspectives on your strengths and areas for improvement. Engage in self-reflection, celebrating your accomplishments and learning from your setbacks. By cultivating self-awareness, you can continually refine your abilities and adapt to new challenges. There are no failures, only learning opportunities. As Bob Ross would put it... "We don't make mistakes, just happy little accidents."

Envision the limitless potential that lies within you. Embrace the belief that there are no limits to what you can achieve when you dedicate yourself to continuous learning and growth. With each new skill you acquire, each insight you gain, and each challenge you overcome, you unlock a deeper layer of your potential, propelling yourself closer to extraordinary success.

By diving into training and personal development, you're making an invaluable investment in yourself—the most significant asset you possess. Through a commitment to lifelong learning, honing your skills, forging meaningful collaborations, embracing feedback, and following a tailored growth plan, you're laying the groundwork for extraordinary personal evolution and achievement. Remember, your development is not only vital for your personal growth but also essential for the success of The Company of You as a whole.

As you nurture your talents and expand your knowledge, you become a catalyst for positive change within your community. Your growth inspires others, creating a culture of continuous improvement that elevates the collective potential of everyone involved. Together, we become a force to be reckoned with, continually pushing the boundaries of what is possible.

Keep in mind that your growth is one of the largest ongoing commitments you'll make in your life. Embrace the mindset of infinite learning, for it is within this mindset that you will find the keys to unlocking your unlimited potential. And you do have unlimited potential – believe that!

Personal Growth Plans

Within The Company of You the importance of personal growth plans cannot be overstated. These plans are your roadmaps that guide and shape your development journey. We use these to ensure that you are continuously progressing towards your goals and aspirations.

A personal growth plan serves as a compass, helping you navigate the vast landscape of self-improvement. It provides clarity on where you are, where you want to be, and the steps required to bridge the gap. Here are some ideas to consider when creating your personal growth plan within The Company of You:

Define Your Vision: Begin by articulating a compelling vision for your future. What does success look like to you? What are your most cherished dreams and aspirations? Clarifying your vision provides a clear direction for your growth and allows you to align your efforts with your desired outcomes.

Keep Meaningful Goals: Break down your vision into actionable and measurable goals. Ensure that your goals are specific, realistic, and time bound. By setting clear targets, you create a sense of purpose and focus that propels you forward. Consider both short-term and long-term goals and identify milestones to celebrate along the way.

Identify Areas for Improvement: Reflect on your strengths and weaknesses, seeking opportunities for growth and development. Pinpoint areas where you would like to enhance your knowledge, skills, or abilities. Consider both professional and personal aspects of your life, such as communication skills, leadership abilities, emotional intelligence, or wellness practices.

Cultivate New Habits: Explore the habits that align with your growth goals and incorporate them into your daily routine. Focus on positive habits that support your physical, mental, and emotional well-being. These could include reading, journaling, exercise, mindfulness practices, or networking activities. By consciously cultivating these habits, you create a solid foundation for ongoing growth.

Seek Learning Opportunities: Engage in continuous learning through various avenues. Attend workshops, seminars, and conferences related to your areas of interest. Enroll in online courses or pursue higher education to deepen your knowledge and expertise. Additionally, seek out mentors, coaches, or industry experts who can provide guidance and support on your growth journey.

Evaluate and Adjust: Regularly assess your progress and reassess your goals and priorities. Take time to reflect on your achievements, challenges, and lessons learned. Celebrate your successes and use setbacks as opportunities for growth and course correction. Remember, personal growth is a dynamic and iterative process that requires ongoing evaluation and adjustment.

As you develop your personal growth plan, ensure that it remains flexible and adaptable. Life is filled with unexpected twists and turns, and your plan should be able to accommodate changes and evolving circumstances. Embrace challenges as opportunities for growth and approach your personal growth plan with a growth mindset.

Within The Company of You your personal growth plan is an invaluable tool that empowers you to take charge of your development. It allows you to cultivate your abilities, embrace opportunities for growth, and make a lasting impact on your life and the lives of those around you.

3

Personal Brand Management

Crafting Your Personal Identity

As the CEO, it's essential to craft a powerful personal brand that authentically reflects your unique qualities, values, and aspirations. Your personal brand serves as the public identity and has significant influence over your personal and professional network.

The pivotal components of brand management are the definition of your brand and the harmonization of your message, your 'why'.

⬤ MESSAGES   now

Mr. Italian
You become a reflection of not only yourself throughout life, but of those who you associate with and work with, as well. Your personal brand is just as much a representation of you as it is those who spend their time with you. This goes both ways.

Defining Your Brand:

Your personal brand is the specific amalgamation of your skills, experiences, values, and passions that distinguish you from others. Defining your brand is a pivotal and continual process that demands self-reflection, a clear sense of purpose, and a profound comprehension of the individuals you aim to engage with and impact. Our chief aim here is to delve into the technical facets of personal branding while infusing it with the very essence of your soul, crafting a more authentic and captivating image.

Now, let's engage in deep introspection and assess your

strengths, talents, experiences, and passions you have uncovered throughout the beginning of this book. These are the bedrock of your personal brand and offer a sturdy basis for constructing an authentic and influential image. Throughout this process, concentrate on what genuinely sparks your soul and consider how you can channel that vitality to inspire and establish a connection with your intended audience.

As you dive into your values and aspirations, ponder the broader ramifications of your personal and professional objectives. How do your values and aspirations harmonize with your distinct qualities and talents?

Identifying your target audience is another indispensable facet of personal branding. To establish meaningful connections, you must initially grasp their needs, preferences, and expectations. Immerse yourself in the intricacies of their lives and aspirations, empathize with their struggles, and align your personal brand with their distinctive viewpoints. By doing this, you create the buy in from others into your brand.

Developing a personal brand statement demands eloquence and the skill to encapsulate your unique essence concisely and memorably. Your statement should not *merely* convey your distinct value proposition but also evoke the essence and ardor that underpin your personal brand. This potent amalgamation will stir your audience and etch an enduring impression on their hearts and minds.

Ensuring consistency in your personal brand is also pivotal for building trust and credibility. Consistency goes beyond your messaging and actions; it includes your online or physical presence, tone of voice, and general demeanor. By upholding a unified and authentic portrayal across all channels of your personal brand, you will create a lasting level of trust with your intended audience. Tackling personal branding with technical precision and infusing it with the very essence of your soul constructs a potent, genuine, and captivating image that goes beyond surface-level interactions and connections with others.

> *"Everyone has a personal brand – by design or by default."*
> *-Lida Citroën*

Consistency plays a pivotal role in the development of your personal brand. It's essential to ensure that your message remains coherent across all channels, which encompass social media, your personal website, and your interactions. This alignment of your message serves as a cornerstone.

To effectively align your message, it's important to conduct a comprehensive audit of your online presence. This involves evaluating your social media accounts, personal website (If you do not have a personal website, I strongly suggest building one), and other online platforms to make sure your content, visuals, and messaging stays consistent and reflects your personal brand in the same light. Maintaining a cohesive visual identity not only enhances brand recognition but also provides a seamless experience for your fans and consumers. Adapting your communication style to suit different platforms, all while maintaining a consistent tone and voice, is the strategy. This requires a nuanced understanding of the unique attributes of each platform and the expectations of its audience. For instance, LinkedIn might necessitate a more professional tone, whereas Instagram may embrace a more informal and visually oriented approach.

Nonetheless, the core message and essence of your

personal brand should maintain consistent across all channels to ensure a recognizable and followable presence.

Leveraging storytelling to convey your brand remains a powerful and engaging technique. By sharing stories that highlight your skills, values, and expertise, you can captivate your audience and provide them with a deeper insight into your distinctive attributes. This approach also allows you to demonstrate your knowledge and experiences in a relatable and memorable manner, thus further strengthening your personal brand.

Authentic engagement is the bedrock of successful personal branding. Active participation in discussions, networking events, and other opportunities to connect with your target audience not only showcases competence and expertise, but also demonstrates dedication to their interests. This proactive approach keeps you informed about industry trends and insights, further enhancing your personal brand's value proposition.

Cultivating relationships with others constitutes a strategic, long-term investment in the growth and success of The Company of You. These relationships not only amplify your professional reputation but also offers invaluable resources and opportunities for collaboration and compounding growth. Community is what truly binds us, and builds us.

Aligning your message stands as a pivotal element in constructing a compelling a full-featured personal brand. Thoroughly auditing your online presence, adapting your communication style, incorporating storytelling, engaging authentically, and fostering relationships all contribute to forging a consistent and captivating personal brand that resonates with your intended audience.

Creating a Powerful Reputation

A powerful reputation is a precious asset.

As we discussed before, the heart of establishing a solid reputation comes from the consistent delivery of exceptional work and a deep understanding of your audience. It's more than just completing tasks—it's about consistently striving for excellence in everything you do.

Research consistently shows that individuals and organizations known for delivering high-quality work tend to attract more clients, customers, and opportunities. When you consistently deliver work that reflects your skills and expertise, you not only demonstrate your competence but also build trust and reliability with others, forming the foundation for a strong reputation.

Understanding your audience is crucial in creating work that truly resonates with them. Conducting market research and audience analysis can provide valuable insights into their needs, preferences, and challenges. Armed with this knowledge, you can tailor your work to address their specific needs and preferences effectively. This empathetic approach not only strengthens your connection with your audience but also positions you as someone who genuinely cares about their well-being.

Integrity is another fundamental building block of a strong reputation. Embracing your core values and carrying yourself with honesty, transparency, and respect in every situation nurtures a sense of trustworthiness and reliability.

Accepting feedback isn't always easy, but it's an essential for growth as individuals. When we open ourselves up to constructive criticism, we're acknowledging that there's room for improvement – and that's okay. It's about recognizing that none of us have all the answers, and that by listening to others, we can gain valuable insights that help us become better versions of ourselves. It's not always comfortable to hear where we've done wrong, but it's in those moments of discomfort that real growth happens.

Learning from the experiences and perspectives of those around us is also crucial for our development. Each person we encounter has their own unique insights and lessons to offer, and by actively listening and engaging with them, we can expand our understanding of the world. Whether it's a mentor sharing their wisdom or a friend offering a different perspective, every interaction has the potential to teach us something new. It's through these exchanges that we broaden our horizons and deepen our understanding of ourselves and others.

Acknowledging the support and contributions of others should be at the top of your list if your goal is to create a supportive and nurturing environment for growth. None of us achieve success on our own – it's often the result of the encouragement, guidance, and assistance of those around us. By expressing gratitude and humility we strengthen our relationships and create a sense of camaraderie and mutual respect. It's about recognizing that we're all in this together, and that by lifting each other up, we can all reach new heights of personal and collective growth.

To broaden your reach and inspire engagement, share your activism journey on social media and other platforms. Build in public. Utilize your personal brand as a catalyst to empower people to get involved, fostering a sense of unity and collaboration around the issues that matter most. Your authentic commitment to positive change will not only benefit your community and industry but also enhance your personal brand's reputation as a force for good.

When you begin to weave these elements into your activism effort; you not only demonstrate your commitment to making a significant impact; but also reinforce a powerful personal brand that sets you apart from others.

When you implement these strategies and concentrate on public relations and activism, you will amplify your voice and presence, enabling you to forge a formidable reputation. With a substantial personal brand presence and an unwavering commitment to making a difference, you will be well-prepared to navigate the complexities of your personal and professional life.

4

Architecting Your Personal Brand's Vision

Your principal aim is to establish a distinct vision and formulate a well-structured path to success by aligning your personal brand, values, and aspirations with both long-term objectives and actionable short-term milestones. As the CEO, you must acknowledge this fact; that progress is an ongoing journey, and it demands both immediate focus and long-term strategizing.

Let's break down some things to think about while you're long-term goalsetting.

A SWOT Analysis: Analyze your strengths, weaknesses, opportunities, and threats to attain a more profound comprehension of your present situation and recognize areas for enhancement and development.

Your Value Proposition: Define the unique combination of skills, expertise, and traits that differentiate you from others. This will lay the groundwork. for your personal brand and assist you in setting goals that correspond with your core competencies.

Your Goal-setting Framework: identify a framework that works for you. Utilize logical systems like the Visionary Equation to establish well defined long-term and agile goals.

Having established your long-term goals, break them down into actionable short-term milestones using the following:

Reverse Engineering: Work backward from your long-term goals to identify the steps required to achieve them. This process will help you. create a series of short-term milestones that align with your long-term objectives and personal brand.

Prioritization Matrix: Assess the urgency and impact of each short-term milestone to prioritize your efforts effectively. Focus on milestones with the highest impact and urgency first.

Progress Tracking: Establish a system to monitor your progress toward each milestone. Regularly review and adjust your approach as needed to ensure continued alignment with your long-term goals and personal brand.

Embrace a comprehensive and flexible approach when formulating your objectives, considering personal and professional aspirations, financial goals, and other factors that might impact your success.

Stay open to the prospect of revisiting and adapting your objectives considering evolving situations or fresh insights. With a well-defined vision and attainable milestones, you'll be well-prepared to make steady strides toward attaining success in both your personal and professional life.

The Visionary Equation

When developing a comprehensive long-term vision, consider the Visionary Equation:

Personal Introspection (PI) + Ambitious Goal setting (AG) + Strategic Thinking (ST) = **Vision (V)**

This equation represents a three-pronged approach that encompasses personal introspection, ambitious goal-setting, and strategic thinking.

Personal Introspection (PI): Throughout our exploration in previous chapters, we've delved into the concept of PI. It's a journey of self-discovery that begins by examining your core values, passions, and the legacy you hope to leave behind. Inspired by influential self-help literature that emphasizes building meaningful connections with others, you reflect on your fundamental principles. This introspective process allows you to construct a long-term vision that resonates with your genuine self, providing a strong foundation for your future endeavors.

Ambitious Goal setting (AG): Inspired by the principles of exponential growth advocated by entrepreneurship experts, establish bold yet attainable goals that harmonize with your personal brand and values. By challenging yourself to achieve greatness, you can unlock your full potential while maintaining congruence with your personal brand and values.

Strategic Thinking (ST): Adopt progressive business philosophies that encourage embracing change and uncertainty. Identify potential obstacles and opportunities, then develop strategies to address challenges and capitalize on favorable circumstances. Understanding that the path to success is often nonlinear and riddled with unexpected hurdles, cultivate a flexible and adaptive mindset to navigate the complexities of your journey.

By employing the Visionary Equation *(V = PI + AG + ST)*, you will be understandingly equipped to embark on your journey of personal and professional growth that harmonizes with your personal brand, and values.

With a strong and self-captivating long-term vision established, you can maintain concentration on your objectives, make informed decisions, and attain long-term success in both your personal and professional missions.

"If you fail to plan, you are planning to fail."
-Alan Lakein

Constructing Short-Term Milestones

It is of critical importance to understand and use short-term milestones. The Synergistic Achievement Lattice in the following text is an approach to breaking down your long-term vision into manageable, attainable steps.

The Synergistic Achievement Lattice

The Synergistic Achievement Lattice is a forward-thinking framework that connects the principles of targeted goal setting, strategic prioritization, and continuous optimization to construct a robust and agile roadmap to success.

Targeted Goal setting: The first layer of the Synergistic Achievement Lattice involves designing a series of granular, quantifiable, feasible, pertinent, and deadline oriented (GQFPD) objectives. These objectives should be meticulously crafted to advance your long-term vision while remaining within the realm of attainability.

$$GQFPD\ Objectives = Granularity \times Quantifiability \times Feasibility \times Pertinence \times Deadline\text{-}orientation$$

Strategic Prioritization: The second layer of the Synergistic Achievement Lattice requires you to assess the significance and potential impact of each goal. By prioritizing your goals based on their strategic value, you can concentrate your efforts on high-impact milestones, effectively allocating your resources for maximum results.

Priority Index (PI) = Strategic Value × Potential Impact

Continuous Optimization: The third layer of the Synergistic Achievement Lattice is the dynamic process of evaluation and adaptation. This iterative approach ensures your short-term milestones remain aligned with your long-term vision and are designed to accommodate evolving circumstances.

By embracing adaptability, you can pivot when necessary and stay on course towards your ultimate objectives.

The Synergistic Achievement Lattice *(Targeted Goal setting, Strategic Prioritization, Continuous Optimization)* provides a new approach for establishing short-term milestones that align with your personal brand and long-term vision.

Bring a malleable mind when adopting this framework, it is no easy task, but it will equip you with the motivation, focus, and adaptability necessary to make steady progress towards your goals.

Implementing the Synergistic Achievement Lattice

To effectively implement the Synergistic Achievement Lattice in your personal branding journey, follow these steps:

Step 1: Define your long-term vision.

- Begin by establishing a clear long-term vision that encapsulates your core values, passions, and the legacy you wish to create. This vision will serve as the foundation upon which you build your Synergistic Achievement Lattice.

Step 2: Develop GQFPD objectives.

- Break down your long-term vision into granular, quantifiable, feasible, and deadline oriented (GQFPD) objectives. Ensure that these objectives are specific, measurable, achievable, relevant, and time efficient.

Step 3: Calculate the Priority Index (PI) for each objective.

- Assess the strategic value and potential impact of each objective.
- Calculate the Priority Index (PI) using the equation: $PI = \text{Strategic Value} \times \text{Potential Impact}$.
- Rank your objectives based on their PI scores, with higher scores indicating higher priority.

Step 4: Continuously monitor and optimize your long-term objectives.

- Regularly evaluate the progress of your objectives and adjust as needed to accommodate evolving circumstances.

Calculate the Optimization Ratio (OR) using the equation: OR = (Realigned Milestones / Total Milestones) × 100.

- Strive to maintain a high OR, which signifies adaptability and agility in your mission.

Example: Using the Synergistic Achievement Lattice for Personal Branding

Long-term vision: Become a renowned motivational speaker in five years, inspiring millions worldwide through live events, books, and online content.

GQFPD Objective 1:

- **Granularity:** Host one motivational event per month.
- **Quantifiability:** Reach 200 attendees per event.
- **Feasibility:** Start with local venues and expand gradually.
- **Pertinence:** Directly aligned with the long-term

vision.

- **Deadline-orientation:** Achieve this within one year.

GQFPD Objective 2:

- **Granularity:** Write and publish a motivational book.
- **Quantifiability:** Sell 10,000 copies in the first year.
- **Feasibility:** Collaborate with a reputable publisher.
- **Pertinence:** Supports the long-term vision.
- **Deadline-orientation:** Launch the book within two years.

Priority Index:

- **For Objective 1:** Strategic Value (7/10) × Potential Impact (8/10) = PI of 56
- **For Objective 2:** Strategic Value (9/10) × Potential Impact (9/10) = PI of 81

Based on the PI scores, Objective 2 (publishing a motivational book) should be prioritized over Objective 1 (hosting motivational events).

Continuous Optimization:

- After six months, you find that hosting one event per month is not feasible due to time constraints. You decide to realign the objective to host one event every two months.

Optimization Ratio (OR) = (1 Realigned Milestone / 2 Total Milestones) × 100 = 50%

By implementing the Synergistic Achievement Lattice and following these guidelines, you create a tailored roadmap to success that works to align your personal brand and long-term vision. Assessing variables in a quantitative way requires assigning numerical values to each variable based on specific criteria or scales.

Below are explanations and examples for each variable within the Synergistic Achievement Lattice framework:

Strategic Value (SV): Assess the strategic value of an objective by considering its alignment with your long-term vision and its potential to contribute to your overall success.

Assign a numerical value from 1 to 10, with 10 representing perfect alignment and high strategic importance.

Example: Objective - Launching a podcast about personal

growth.

If your long-term vision is to become a renowned motivational speaker, launching a podcast on personal growth has strong alignment and contributes to your overall success. Thus, you might assign an SV of 8.

Potential Impact (PI): Evaluate the potential impact of an objective by estimating the extent to which it can positively affect your target audience, market, or industry. Assign a numerical value from 1 to 10, with 10 representing a significant positive impact.

Example: Objective - Writing a blog post about goal-setting techniques.

If your target audience is people seeking personal growth, a blog post about goal-setting techniques could have a moderate impact on your readers. if you have readers, you might assign a PI of 6.

Granularity (G): Granularity refers to the level of detail or specificity of an objective. When quantifying granularity, consider how clearly an objective outlines the tasks or actions needed to achieve it.

Assign a numerical value from 1 to 10, with 10 representing the highest level of specificity.

Example: Objective - Increase social media presence.

This objective is relatively broad and lacks specificity. For this you might assign a G of 3.

Quantifiability (Q): Quantifiability refers to the measurability of an objective. To quantify this variable, assess how easily an objective can be measured in terms of progress and results. Assign a numerical value from 1 to 10, with 10 representing the highest level of measurability.

Example: Objective - Gain 5,000 new followers on Instagram within six months.

This objective is easily measurable, as you can track your progress and results using Instagram's analytics. Thus, you might assign a Q of 9.

Feasibility (F): Feasibility refers to the likelihood of successfully achieving an objective given your available resources, time, and constraints. Assign a numerical value from 1 to 10, with 10 representing the highest level of feasibility.

Example: Objective - Publish a book within two months.

If you have limited time and have not yet started writing the book, this objective might be challenging to achieve. In this case, you might assign an F of 2.

Pertinence (P): Pertinence refers to the relevance of an objective to your long-term vision, personal brand, or values. To quantify, assign a numerical value from 1 to 10, with 10 representing the highest level of relevance.

Example: Objective - Attend a personal branding workshop.

If your long-term vision is to build a strong personal brand, attending a personal branding workshop is highly relevant. Here, you might assign a P of 9.

Deadline-orientation (D): Deadline-orientation refers to the time-bound nature of an objective. Assess the degree to which an objective has a clear and realistic deadline. Assign a numerical value from 1 to 10, with 10 representing the highest level of deadline orientation.

Example: Objective - Complete an online course on public speaking by the end of the month.

If the course has a well-defined curriculum, this objective has a clear and realistic deadline. You might assign a D of 8.

By quantifying each variable, you can use the Synergistic Achievement Lattice framework to assess and prioritize your objectives more effectively. Once you have assigned numerical values to all variables for each objective, you can calculate the overall score for each objective using the logical equation:

Overall Score (OS) = SV * PI * G * Q * F * P * D

This equation computes the overall score by multiplying

the values of each variable. The higher the overall score, the more aligned and beneficial the objective is to your long-term vision and personal brand. Let's revisit the examples we discussed earlier:

Launching a podcast about personal growth:
SV = 8, PI = 6, G = 7, Q = 8, F = 7, P = 8, D = 7
OS = 8 * 6 * 7 * 8 * 7 * 8 * 7 = 84,672

Writing a blog post about goal-setting techniques:
SV = 5, PI = 6, G = 6, Q = 7, F = 9, P = 6, D = 8
OS = 5 * 6 * 6 * 7 * 9 * 6 * 8 = 30,240

Increase social media presence:

$SV = 7, PI = 6, G = 3, Q = 7, F = 8, P = 6, D = 5$

$OS = 7 * 6 * 3 * 7 * 8 * 6 * 5 = 17,640$

Gain 5,000 new followers on Instagram within six months:

$SV = 6, PI = 7, G = 8, Q = 9, F = 7, P = 7, D = 9$

$OS = 6 * 7 * 8 * 9 * 7 * 7 * 9 = 120,960$

Publish a book within two months:

$SV = 8, PI = 8, G = 7, Q = 8, F = 2, P = 9, D = 4$

$OS = 8 * 8 * 7 * 8 * 2 * 9 * 4 = 25,344$

Attend a personal branding workshop:

$SV = 7, PI = 6, G = 9, Q = 7, F = 9, P = 9, D = 8$

$OS = 7 * 6 * 9 * 7 * 9 * 9 * 8 = 197,424$

After calculating the overall scores for each objective, you can prioritize them based on the highest overall scores. In this example, the objectives with the highest overall scores are:

1. Attend a personal branding workshop (197,424)
2. Gain 5,000 new followers on Instagram within six months (120,960)
3. Launching a podcast about personal growth (84,672)

After assessing each variable in a quantitative way, you can make more informed decisions about which objectives to focus on and allocate your resources accordingly.

This approach helps you prioritize tasks that are most aligned with your long-term vision and personal brand, increasing the likelihood of achieving your goals.

With the prioritized objectives in hand, you can now create a strategic plan to achieve these goals by allocating your resources, time, and energy effectively.

Here's how you can develop an action plan for the top three objectives based on the Synergistic Achievement Lattice framework:

Attend a personal branding workshop (OS = 197,424):

- Research and identify the most relevant workshops or conferences focused on personal branding.
- Plan your schedule and budget to accommodate the attendance of the chosen workshop.
- Connect with workshop organizers, presenters, and attendees to network and learn from their experiences.

Gain 5,000 new followers on Instagram within six months (OS = 120,960):

- Develop a content strategy for your Instagram

profile that is consistent with your personal brand and values.

- Engage with your target audience by posting relevant, high-quality content and responding to comments and messages.
- Utilize Instagram growth strategies such as collaborations, influencer partnerships, and sponsored posts to reach a wider audience.

Launch a podcast about personal growth (OS = 84,672):

- Identify your podcast's niche, target audience, and key topics related to personal growth.
- Invest in the necessary equipment and software for high-quality audio recording and editing.
- Market your podcast through social media, email, and collaborate with other podcasters or influencers in your niche.

By developing a detailed action plan for each prioritized objective, you can ensure that you are making consistent progress toward your long-term vision. Regularly reviewing your progress and recalibrating your short-term milestones as needed will help you stay on track and maintain momentum.

Remember that the Synergistic Achievement Lattice

framework is a dynamic tool that can be adjusted and refined as you gain new insights and experiences. Continuously evaluate and update the values for each variable, and recalculate the overall scores as needed to ensure that your objectives remain aligned with your long-term vision and personal brand.

Once you have gathered the data, calculated the overall scores, and prioritized your objectives using the Synergistic Achievement Lattice framework, the next step is to put your plan into action and monitor your progress.

Here's how to proceed:

Implement your action plan: Start executing the action plan for each prioritized objective. This may involve allocating resources, setting deadlines, and defining intermediate milestones to measure progress. Stay committed to your plan but be prepared to adjust when necessary.

Monitor progress and outcomes: Regularly review your progress towards each short-term milestone and long-term objective. Track relevant metrics and indicators (e.g., the number of new followers, podcast downloads, or workshop learnings) to measure the effectiveness of your actions and strategies.

Adjust and refine: Based on your progress and the

outcomes you observe, make necessary adjustments to your strategies, resource allocation, or timeline. Update the values for the four variables in the framework (Personal Importance, Achievability, Time Sensitivity, and Resource Intensity) as needed.

Reassess and reprioritize: Periodically reassess your objectives and overall scores, especially if there have been significant changes in your personal or professional life. Adjust your priorities and action plans accordingly to ensure that your short-term milestones remain aligned with your long-term vision and personal brand.

Reflect and learn: Take the time to reflect on your experiences, successes, and challenges. Identify key lessons and insights gained from your personal branding journey and apply them to future endeavors. This continuous learning process will help you grow and improve, both personally and professionally. By following these steps, you can effectively use the Synergistic Achievement Lattice framework to guide your personal branding efforts and achieve your goals. This iterative process encourages adaptability, continuous improvement, and strategic decision-making, enabling you to make a lasting impact in your personal and professional life.

By developing a detailed action plan for each prioritized objective, you can ensure consistent progress toward your long-term vision. However, to stay on track and maintain momentum, it's essential to not only execute but also monitor your progress effectively.

This brings us to the next critical component: **objective tracking**. To ensure that you are consistently aligned with your vision, you need a system to evaluate and adjust your actions. A clear and structured method for tracking objectives will help you allocate resources efficiently, prioritize tasks effectively, and maintain focus on what truly matters.

To make this process manageable, you can create an **Objective Tracking Table** that quantifies key variables such as **Personal Importance**, **Achievability**, **Time Sensitivity**, and **Resource Intensity**. This table will provide a visual guide to help you reassess, reprioritize, and reflect on your progress. Here's how it works:

Objective	Personal Importance (1-10)	Achievability (1-10)	Time Sensitivity (1-10)	Resource Intensity (1-10)	Overall Score	Priority

Fill in the objectives: In the first column, list your short-term milestones and long-term objectives related to your personal brand.

Rate the variables: For each objective, rate the Personal Importance, Achievability, Time Sensitivity, and Resource

Intensity on a scale of 1 to 10.

Calculate the overall score: The overall score for each objective is calculated by multiplying Personal Importance, Achievability, and Time Sensitivity, then dividing by the square of Resource Intensity. This formula prioritizes tasks that are important, achievable, and urgent while strongly penalizing those that require more resources, encouraging efficiency in goal setting.

Overall Score

$$\frac{Personal\ Importance\ x\ Achieveability\ x\ Time\ Sensitivity}{Resource\ Intensity}$$

Determine the priority: Sort the objectives by their overall scores in descending order. Assign priority rankings based on the sorted scores, with the highest score receiving the top priority.

Monitor progress: As you work on your objectives and make progress, update the table with new data, such as changes in the ratings for the four variables or the addition of new objectives.

Reassess and reprioritize: Periodically reassess your objectives and overall scores, adjusting the priorities and action plans as needed to ensure alignment with your long-term vision and personal brand.

Reflect and learn: Use the table to reflect on your experiences, successes, and challenges, identifying key lessons and insights to apply to future endeavors.

Below is an example of a table with data for a business coach using the Synergistic Achievement Lattice framework:

Objective	Personal Importance (1-10)	Achievability (1-10)	Time Sensitivity (1-10)	Resource Intensity (1-10)	Overall Score	Priority
Attend Networking Events	8	7	6	3	37.33	1
Create a social media presence	8	8	7	4	28.00	2
Launch coaching website	9	8	7	5	20.16	3
Write e-book on business growth	7	6	4	4	10.5	4
Develop coaching program	10	7	5	6	19.72	5

**In this example, the business coach has identified five objectives and rated each one based on the four variables: Personal Importance, Achievability, Time Sensitivity, and Resource Intensity. The overall scores have been calculated, and the priorities have been assigned accordingly. By using this table, the business coach can focus on the most important objectives and track their progress over time.

Executing Your Plan

Transitioning from building a strong support system and establishing a robust strategy, it's essential to understand how project management principles can be applied to effectively execute plans and achieve goals.

Let's explore these principles further; The importance of monitoring progress, overcoming challenges, and the significance of activism for positive change.

Project management principles offer a structured approach to executing plans and achieving goals. When we break down objectives into smaller, manageable tasks, we can ensure that your efforts remain focused and aligned with our overall vision. Additionally, by assigning deadlines and allocating resources to each task, we can maintain a realistic timeline for progress and minimize the risk of delays or setbacks.

Monitoring progress regularly is crucial to ensure that you stay on track and can promptly address any issues that may arise. By evaluating your performance against established benchmarks, you can identify areas for improvement and adjust your strategy accordingly. It's essential to maintain a flexible mindset and adapt your approach as needed to respond to new information, changing circumstances, or unforeseen challenges.

In a world that operates on deadlines, budgets, and strategic goals, a project manager serves as the guiding force, seamlessly aligning resources and timelines to bring a project to fruition. They track progress, tackle obstacles, and ensure that every piece of the project puzzle aligns with the broader vision. This very principle can be applied to the journey of self-actualization - a voyage towards becoming the best version of oneself.

To begin, let's consider self-actualization as our project. It is our grand vision, the pinnacle of personal achievement and fulfillment. The path towards self-actualization can be visualized as a series of tasks or milestones, each leading us closer to our ultimate objective. But how does one monitor the progress of such a deeply personal and abstract project? The answer lies in:

...strategic planning

regular check-ins

tracking milestones

resilience in the face of obstacles

and normalize celebrating successes...

Strategic Planning: Begin by setting specific, measurable, achievable, relevant, and time-bound (SMART) goals.

These will function as your key performance indicators (KPIs) to measure your progress on your self-actualization journey. The goals could involve:

...developing a particular skill,
enhancing emotional intelligence,
nurturing healthier relationships,
or attaining work-life balance...

Remember, your goals should profoundly align with your personal aspirations and values.

Regular Check-ins: Regard these goals as 'mini projects' within your self-actualization journey. Schedule regular check-ins with yourself, just as a project manager would conduct project reviews. Utilize these moments to assess whether your actions align with your broader vision.

Do your actions reflect your core values?

Are you making progress towards your goals?

Addressing these questions will assist you in identifying if you're veering off track and enable you to adjust your path accordingly.

Milestone Tracking: Break down your goals into smaller tasks or milestones and monitor your completion of these milestones. This provides a tangible structure to your self-actualization journey and allows you to visualize your progress.

For instance, if your goal is to lead a healthier lifestyle, milestones could include daily exercise, increased consumption of fruits and vegetables, or achieving a healthier body mass index.

Resilience in Face of Obstacles: Just as any project faces unforeseen challenges, your journey will also encounter obstacles. These could be external, like financial constraints, or internal, like self-doubt or fear of failure.

Treat these obstacles as you would in a project:

Scenario –

...identify the problem,

explore possible solutions,

and implement a remedial strategy.

Remember, resilience and adaptability are key...

Finally, commemorate your accomplishments, regardless of their size. Every milestone attained, each goal reached, and each obstacle surmounted deserves acknowledgment. Let celebrations be a part of your motivation.

Your end goal is not a destination but an ongoing project, a continuous process of growth and evolution. Like an adept project manager, embrace the practice of monitoring your progress, adapting to changes, and persevering towards your objectives. Remember, the crux of effective project management and self-actualization lies in recognizing that progress, not perfection, is the aim.

You are a work in progress, striving each day to become a better version of yourself, to attain the highest level of your potential, and to realize your personal vision of success.

As we transition into the practical application of the concepts we've discussed, I present a unique, proprietary approach to monitoring and guiding your journey of personal growth and self-actualization – the A.C.T.I.V.A.T.E Method.

Assess: The first step on this journey is to conduct a comprehensive inventory of your current state, much like an organization carries out a thorough audit before strategic planning. Identifying your strengths, weaknesses, passions, and fears provides you with a clear picture of your standing and the aspects you need to work on for personal growth.

Create: Armed with your self-assessment, you're prepared to set precise, challenging, yet achievable goals. These goals should deeply resonate with your core values and align with your broader vision of self-actualization, serving as the roadmap for your personal growth journey.

Timeline: Establishing a clear timeline for each goal infuses your journey with a sense of urgency and purpose. A defined end-date sparks motivation, functioning as a call-to-action for your aspirations.

Integrate: To ensure continuous progress, it's essential to integrate your goals into the fabric of your daily life. Break down your goals into smaller, manageable tasks that seamlessly fit into your everyday routine.

Visualize: Harness the power of your mind by regularly visualizing your success. Envision yourself achieving your goals and be excited about the new limits you can push with the next set of goals.

Adapt: Remain open and flexible. If a strategy doesn't yield the expected results, don't hesitate to adapt and modify your approach. Resilience and adaptability serve as your allies on this journey.

Track: Tracking your progress is crucial to maintaining focus and commitment. Utilize a journal, an app, or a simple calendar to record your accomplishments, setbacks, and insights along the way.

Evaluate: At predetermined intervals, pause to evaluate your progress. Celebrate your successes, learn from your setbacks, and reevaluate your strategies if necessary. Recall, progress, not perfection, is the goal.

Incorporating the A.C.T.I.V.A.T.E Method into your life acts as a catalyst, propelling you towards your self-actualization goals. It encourages active participation, regular evaluation, and consistent action towards personal growth and development. As you continue to navigate the complexities of your personal and professional life, remember, the power to shape your future is in your hands. It's time to A.C.T.I.V.A.T.E your potential and become the CEO of your life.

Overcoming Challenges

Overcoming challenges and setbacks is an inevitable part of the journey toward achieving your goals. Developing resilience and a growth mindset will enable you to view these challenges as opportunities for learning and growth. By seeking support from your network, mentors, and advisors, you can leverage their expertise and experience to develop effective strategies to overcome obstacles and continue moving forward. Moreover, it's vital to recognize the significance of activism for positive change and explore ways to incorporate it into your personal and professional life. By leveraging your unique strengths and talents, you can make a meaningful difference in the world and demonstrate your commitment to creating a better future.

Whether you choose to champion a specific cause, volunteer your time, or advocate for policy changes, your activism can significantly impact your personal brand and establish you as a leader in your field.

There's no personal growth without challenge. As you chart your journey using the A.C.T.I.V.A.T.E method, expect to encounter setbacks and hurdles. The goal isn't to avoid these challenges but to equip yourself with the skills and mindset to overcome them.

Sometimes, the challenges may seem overwhelming, but

remember, you're not alone. Let me emphasize the significance of activism as an integral part of your journey. Activism reflects your commitment to change, growth, and impact - core values of a proactive CEO. You have the power to use your unique strengths and talents to make a meaningful difference in the world both for yourself, and others.

Whether it's championing a cause close to your heart, volunteering your time for those in need, or advocating for policy changes in your organization or community, your activism will create ripples of positive change.
This chapter concludes with a strong call to action - face challenges head-on, ignite your passion for positive change, and step into the extraordinary power of being the CEO of your life.

Cultivating resilience is an art, a constant process of learning, unlearning, and relearning. It's like the phoenix rising from the ashes, repeatedly, each time with renewed vigor and deeper wisdom. As you embrace the highs and lows of your journey, remember that it's not about the destination but the transformation you undergo along the way.

Much like the process of developing resilience, the practice of personal activism is also a journey. It's a pathway to finding your voice, standing up for what you believe in, and channeling your experiences, talents, and passions to create a meaningful impact in the world. It can involve volunteering at a local charity, advocating for changes in policies at your workplace, or even using your personal platform to raise awareness about the causes close to your heart.

The intersection of resilience and activism is where magic happens. When you harness the power of your challenges to fuel your journey and view setbacks not as dead ends but as detours leading you toward new possibilities, and you activate the power to create meaningful change.

Throughout this process, remember to stay true to your unique journey. Everyone's path is different, and comparing yours with others will only lead to unnecessary stress and self-doubt. Instead, focus on your personal growth, your achievements, and the positive changes you are making in your life and the world.

Remember, it's not about how fast you get there, but who you are once you arrive.

Let's imagine for a moment that your journey of personal growth is a rollercoaster ride. The rising slopes represent the growth stages, where you're gaining new knowledge, skills, and experiences. The peaks are your moments of success, where you reach your goals and bask in the joy of achievement. The sudden drops and curves, on the other hand, represent the challenges and setbacks. It's a thrilling ride, filled with adrenaline, unexpected twists, and turns, but most importantly, transformative experiences.

Now, resilience is the safety harness on this rollercoaster. It keeps you secure as you navigate the ups and downs, ensuring that the sudden drops don't throw you off the track. It's the reliable safety net that allows you to enjoy the ride with confidence, knowing that you're prepared to handle whatever comes your way.

Continuing the rollercoaster analogy, personal activism is the unique track you're on. It's the path you carve out with your passions, values, and purpose. It's where you decide the direction and speed of your journey, using your strengths and abilities to influence change and make an impact.

And what about the mentors, advisors, and your network? They are the guideposts, the navigation tools, and the friendly voices over the intercom offering guidance and support. They give you valuable insights, alert you to potential obstacles, and cheer you on every step of the way. It is ultimately your decision to always keep your hands and feet inside the car, Afterall. This rollercoaster ride is dynamic, unpredictable, and exhilarating – much like your personal growth journey.

But here's the fun part – you're not just the passenger on this ride; you're also the designer, the operator, and the navigator. You have the power to shape your path, control your speed, and determine your destination. And each twist and turn, each high and low, is an opportunity to learn, grow, and transform.

So, strap on your resilience harness, chart your activism track, and get ready for the thrilling rollercoaster ride of personal growth. Because the real fun lies not in reaching the end of the ride, but in the transformational experience itself.

"Please keep hands, feet, and other objects inside the vehicle at all times - Enjoy the ride!"

5

Asset Analysis

Understanding your value is paramount to ensuring effective allocation of your time and resources. In this section, we will explore methods for appraising the value of your skills, knowledge, and expertise, as well as understanding your standing in the marketplace. Additionally, we will discuss aligning your personal brand with your value proposition to ensure you are effectively communicating your unique value.

The Finance Department of the Company of You isn't exclusively fixated on monetary wealth.

Rather, its focus lies in comprehending and investing in intrinsic value – encompassing your skills, knowledge, talents, experiences, and the distinct value proposition that you contribute to the world. Your intrinsic value stands as your most substantial asset, and nurturing it reaps significant dividends in terms of personal growth, career advancement, and overall life contentment.

Much like a financial analyst would assess a company's value based on diverse assets, liabilities, revenues, and market conditions, you too should regularly evaluate your intrinsic value. While this analysis may not always be simple, it's pivotal for your ongoing growth.

How do you measure your accomplishments?

Begin by establishing concrete, quantifiable goals linked to your personal growth, professional advancement, or specific skills you aim to acquire. Your metrics might involve the count of books read, courses finished, promotions earned, or any other measurable outcomes. Remember, these aren't merely numerical values; they embody your diligent effort, unwavering perseverance, and steadfast commitment. They serve as the "revenues" within your personal finance report.

Yet, the focus isn't solely on figures and growth graphs. At times, authentic accomplishments lie within the journey itself: the hurdles you've surmounted, the challenges you've confronted head-on, the tenacity you've exhibited. These qualitative aspects might not be directly quantifiable, yet they serve as substantial indicators of your growth, equally deserving of acknowledgment and celebration.

Now, let's delve into the "marketplace." In the context of the Company of You, this encompasses your social and professional networks, your industry, and the broader world.

...What value do you contribute?

What's your unique selling proposition?

How does your personal brand stand out?...

Comprehending your value within this marketplace is pivotal, as it influences your relationships, career advancement, and personal contentment. Aligning your personal brand with your value proposition guarantees that your deeds and communications mirror the distinct value you bring.

Comprehending your value is a multifaceted undertaking:

*...demanding introspection,
proactive measures,
and continuous reevaluation...*

However, bear in mind that within the Finance Department of the Company of You, the return on investment transcends monetary gains. It counts for personal growth, contentment, and the gratification of leading an authentic life that harmonizes with your distinctive value.

Intrinsic value isn't a fixed measure; it's dynamic, and evolves with every new skill you acquire, each unique experience you undergo, and each challenge you conquer. Imagine it as a stock who's worth can oscillate based on diverse life 'market' influences. One of the most potent means to enhance this value is through continuous learning and personal development. View each learning opportunity as an investment in yourself.

Whether it involves enrolling in an online course, reading a book, participating in a workshop, or tackling a demanding project at work – all these contribute to your repository of knowledge and skillset, consequently amplifying your intrinsic value.

In the professional realm, the returns from these investments often materialize as career advancements – but also can come in the form of a promotion, a salary increase, a successful project, or the gratification of a job well executed.

Nonetheless, the genuine dividends stretch well beyond the professional domain, yielding augmented self-assurance, expanded viewpoints, and a more enriched, gratifying life.

However, an investment strategy isn't solely about channeling resources into assets. It is also about tracking performance. Formulating clear, measurable goals associated with personal development and meticulously monitoring progress towards these objectives. Consider these questions often:

Did the investments yield the projected returns?

Do any adjustments seem necessary?

This review process is pivotal to gauge your growth, pinpoint areas for enhancement, and strategize for future 'investments'.

Understanding the value of your skills, knowledge, and experiences within the marketplace is also a pivotal aspect.

This evaluation of value often requires an outward perspective. Examine industry trends, sought-after skills, and potential gaps you could bridge.

Subsequently, harmonize your personal development aspirations with these insights to augment your market value.

At the same time, it's important to remember that your value is not solely defined by market demands.

…Your distinctive combination of strengths, passions, and values.

– Your Personal Brand –

Your personal brand introduces an immeasurable yet substantial dimension to your overall worth. Reflecting upon one's value, encompassing both intrinsic and market aspects, isn't a one-time endeavor. It's an ongoing journey of investment, assessment, and refinement.

Investing in yourself, as we've explored, embarks on a multifaceted journey that involves nurturing your capabilities, values, and passions, and weaving these elements into your personal brand. Your personal brand is the factor that sets you apart in a crowded arena.

Evaluating Growth

Evaluating your growth is essential to ensure that you make progress toward your long-term goals and objectives.

By comprehending your value, measuring your accomplishments, and evaluating your growth, you can secure the effective investment of your time and resources within the Company of You.

While the notion of a personal brand may seem inherently external—focused on how others perceive you—it's crucial to remember that it originates from within.

Authenticity in your personal brand emerges from a profound understanding of your values, motivations, and aspirations. Thus, introspection constitutes a pivotal aspect of brand cultivation. Dedicate regular time to reflecting on your experiences and insights gained; practicing this will yield those profound "Ah Ha!" revelations and steer your future growth. Similarly, seeking feedback from others can serve as an invaluable tool for personal growth. Whether it comes from mentors, colleagues, friends, or family, external perspectives can shed light on overlooked strengths or areas for improvement not immediately apparent.

However, while external input can be beneficial, remember that you remain the ultimate decision-maker regarding your personal brand. Your personal brand is intrinsically intertwined with your self-worth. Embracing your unique value proposition can enhance your confidence in navigating personal and professional challenges. A robust personal brand can offer guidance in decision-making, bring clarity to your goals, and influence how you choose to invest in self-improvement.

The journey of comprehending your worth and personal brand go further than just bettering your marketability in an overcrowded market. It's about crafting an authentic, fulfilling life that aligns with your core identity and cherished values.

The task to self-assess and evaluate your growth might seem challenging given the numerous and often deeply personal factors at play. But stay strong, because with a structured approach, this experience transforms into a gratifying exercise.

Assessing your skills and knowledge forms a pragmatic initial step. Creating a foundation of your existing abilities and monitoring their progression aids in visualizing advancements. Reflecting on this journey over time can offer deep insight into your path of growth.

Soliciting feedback from others is another useful tactic. Often, those around us notice our growth even when we fail to see it ourselves. Constructive feedback from trusted colleagues, mentors, or even family and friends can provide external validation of your growth. This external perspective can also highlight areas you may need to focus on, thus serving as a guide for future learning objectives.

Introspection is an invaluable tool in evaluating growth. Personal development often brings about changes in perspectives, values, and even aspirations. Regular self-reflection helps you become aware of these changes. You may notice a shift in how you react to challenges or that you're now able to manage stress more effectively. Perhaps you've become more empathetic or more assertive. Recognizing these subtle changes in your character and mindset is essential as they're often signs of profound personal growth.

One critical thing to remember while evaluating growth is to practice self-compassion. Growth is a gradual process that often happens in fits and starts. There might be periods of rapid progress followed by periods of stagnation, and that's perfectly normal. It's important not to judge yourself harshly during slower periods. Remember, personal development is not a race; it's a lifelong journey.

Understanding your value, measuring your accomplishments, and evaluating your growth are all part of the essential process of investing in the Company of You. They form the basis of the personal balance sheet that allows you to appreciate the return on investment from all your efforts. Assisted by the strategies from the Finance Department of your life, you'll be better equipped to drive personal growth, make informed decisions, and steer your life towards achieving your long-term goals.

Continuing from the topic of personal growth evaluation, it's important to recognize that such evaluation transcends the traditional metrics of success.

Personal growth is multifaceted, encompassing:
- intellectual growth,
- emotional maturity,
- physical wellness,
- spiritual evolution,
- and social development.

Hence, the metrics used to evaluate growth inherently earn this complexity. This multi-dimensional approach to evaluating growth broadens the scope of your self-assessment. Consider emotional growth, for instance – it can be measured by an increased capacity to handle stress or adversity, improved emotional intelligence, or even your ability to establish and maintain healthy relationships. Similarly, intellectual growth can be assessed through the attainment of new knowledge, acquisition of new skills, or improved problem-solving abilities.

Additionally, as part of understanding your value, it's equally important to take stock of your contributions to the world.

Have you made an impact on someone's life?

Have you contributed to your community in meaningful ways?

These accomplishments, often overlooked in traditional success metrics, are significant indicators of personal growth. Just as a company regularly reviews its mission and vision, you too must periodically revisit your personal life's mission and vision. You may discover that with your growth and life experiences, your personal mission has evolved, and new visions have formed. Recognizing this evolution is an integral part of understanding your value and self-worth.

It is important to remember that the path of personal growth, although personal, need not be solitary. Involve trusted individuals from your life in your journey. Their perspectives can offer invaluable insights and aid you in recognizing growth areas you might otherwise overlook.

The journey of growth is ongoing, marked by revelations, accomplishments, and occasional setbacks. Embrace this journey with an open mind and a positive attitude.

6

Process Improvement

Optimizing Your Daily Routine

Welcome to Process Improvement. It is time we strive to streamline for maximum efficiency and balance. The first aspect we'll explore under this department is Process Improvement, with a specific focus on optimizing your daily routine.

This is about creating order from chaos, setting the rhythm of your life in a manner that enhances productivity, reduces stress, and allows you to experience a deep sense of fulfillment and contentment. In life, as in business, time is a precious and non-renewable resource. Yet, all too often, we find ourselves racing against the clock, feeling overwhelmed by a barrage of tasks and responsibilities.

But what if we could change that? What if we could manage our time more effectively, accomplish our tasks more efficiently, and still find time for the things that truly matter to us? This is dedicated to unraveling the art of time management, a vital tool in the kit of every successful CEO. By mastering time management, you will achieve more with less stress. Compounding Efficiency.

The techniques we will explore are not about packing more tasks into your already busy schedule. Instead, they focus on prioritizing your tasks, eliminating unnecessary activities, and streamlining your processes so that you can make the most of your time.

The process improvement expedition begins now. One pivotal facet of this refinement involves identifying your peak productivity periods, harnessing the power of your unique circadian rhythms, which dictate your energy levels and productivity throughout the day. By understanding your moments of peak productivity, you can strategically schedule your most critical tasks to capitalize on heightened focus and energy.

Experimenting with various activities during different times of day will provide invaluable insights into your optimal working hours. For me, I am not an early morning person. My down time is between 2am-8am, optimal hours being 4pm-10pm, and productive hours being 9:30am-3:30pm.

Time Management Techniques

Effective time management is foundational to personal and professional triumph. Within this section, we embark on an exploration of an array of time management methodologies theorized to boost your productivity and enhance your overall well-being.

One technique is the concept of Time Blocking. Time Blocking entails the division of your day into dedicated segments or blocks, each exclusively allocated to a specific task or activity. This approach is firmly rooted in the realms of attention and cognitive psychology, which advocate for optimal brain function when focusing on a single task for an extended period without disruptions.

By dedicating blocks of time to specific tasks or activities, you can minimize distractions and make the most of your limited cognitive resources.

When implementing Time Blocking, consider the following:

- Identify your daily priorities and categorize them by type, such as work tasks, self-care activities, and social commitments.

- Determine the optimal duration for each block of time based on the nature of the task and your personal preferences. Research indicates that working in blocks of 25-50 minutes followed by a short break can help maintain focus and prevent mental fatigue.

- Schedule these blocks of time throughout your day considering your natural energy levels, peak productivity periods, and other commitments.

- Commit to focusing exclusively on the task at hand during each block, minimizing distractions and multitasking.

Incorporating complementary activities into your scheduled breaks during Time Blocking can be a valuable strategy. Engaging in exercises and mindfulness practices during these intervals not only enhances your time management skills but also contributes to the creation of a consistent and healthy proactive routine.

The next technique to explore is the **Pomodoro Technique**, a time management method named after a tomato-shaped kitchen timer. This technique is simple but remarkably effective.

The idea is to break your work into 25-minute chunks, each followed by a 5-minute break. After every fourth "Pomodoro," or 25-minute work period, you take a longer break of 15-30 minutes. It is rumored that Darwin worked best using the Pomodoro technique, and this technique enabled Darwin to accomplish the feats that defined his career, including his groundbreaking work on the theory of evolution. While there's no historical evidence directly linking Darwin to this method, the Pomodoro Technique is widely praised for enhancing focus and productivity.

The structured intervals create a sense of urgency, encouraging you to work with intense concentration during each 25-minute session. The scheduled breaks, on the other hand, allow you to recharge, preventing burnout and maintaining mental clarity throughout the day.

This system is designed to improve mental agility and combat the feeling of burnout. This technique is especially useful for tackling large projects or repetitive tasks that can otherwise feel overwhelming. By focusing on small, manageable intervals, the Pomodoro Technique helps you build momentum and maintain consistent progress.

Whether you're studying, working on creative projects, or managing your daily to-do list, this method can make a significant difference in your productivity.

However, effective time management isn't just about getting more done. It's about getting the right things done, and this is where the Eisenhower Matrix comes in.

This time management tool helps you sort tasks by their urgency and importance, resulting in four categories:

1. Do First
2. Schedule
3. Delegate
4. Don't Do

The Eisenhower Matrix is magic of its ability to help you focus on what truly matters, eliminating non-essential activities that consume your time and energy without contributing to your goals.

Another technique we'll delve into is mindfulness. Although not often associated with time management, mindfulness plays a critical role in enhancing our focus and reducing stress. By practicing mindfulness, you can learn to tune out distractions and be fully present in the moment, thereby improving your efficiency and productivity.

Regularly take stock of your time management practices.

...Are they helping you achieve your goals?
...Are you feeling more balanced?

Continuous evaluation allows you to tweak your methods and adapt them to your evolving needs and goals.

Managing your time is about more than squeezing tasks into every minute of the day. It's about creating a lifestyle that allows for work, rest, AND play. Our goal here is to make sure we are not just existing... but truly living.

Next area that significantly impacts your productivity:
Habits.

The journey to becoming an efficient and balanced CEO of the Company of You isn't only about incorporating beneficial practices into your daily routine, but also about identifying and eliminating the unproductive ones.

Unproductive habits are behaviors that, over time, hinder your progress towards your goals. These might include excessive use of social media, procrastination, a lack of exercise, or even persistently staying up too late without productivity. Such habits drain your time, energy, and focus, leaving you with little to invest in the activities that truly matter. They often serve as comfort zones, preventing you from reaching your full potential.

By the end of this section, you will have a clearer understanding of your behavioral patterns and practical strategies to reshape them. Your commitment to this process is crucial, as small, consistent changes in your habits can have a profound impact on your overall productivity, efficiency, and work-life balance. This step is essential in optimizing the operations of the Company of You, as habits form the foundation of our daily routines.

Are you ready to declutter your life and make space for growth and efficiency? Let's dive in!

Understanding your habits is the first step to altering them. Start by keeping a journal where you can record your activities throughout the day. Over time, patterns will emerge, and you'll be able to identify habits that are counterproductive to your goals. Remember, these could range from major timewasters, like spending hours scrolling aimlessly through social media, to more subtle energy drainers, like unnecessary perfectionism that prevents you from finishing tasks in a timely manner.

Once you've identified your unproductive habits, aim to understand why they exist.

- *Do they provide temporary relief from stress or boredom?*

- *Are they tied to certain triggers in your environment or negative emotional states?*

For instance, if you notice that you often reach for your

phone and browse social media when you're feeling overwhelmed, the habit serves as a distraction from uncomfortable emotions. Awareness of these patterns and triggers is crucial in the process of habit change. With this awareness in hand, you can then begin the work of replacing unproductive habits with more beneficial ones.

This is where the principle of "habit stacking" comes into play. Developed by productivity expert James Clear, habit stacking involves linking a new, beneficial habit to an existing one.

The existing habit acts as a trigger for the new habit, thereby increasing the likelihood of the new habit sticking. For example, if you have a habit of drinking a cup of coffee first thing in the morning, you could stack a new habit of spending five minutes on mindfulness or planning your day onto it. In this way, your morning coffee triggers your new beneficial habit.

Moreover, don't underestimate the power of your environment in shaping your behavior. By consciously designing your environment, you can make productive habits more convenient and unproductive habits more inconvenient.

For instance, if you aim to reduce the time spent on your phone, leaving it in another room while you work could make a significant difference.

Remember, changing habits isn't about immediate results; it's about incremental improvements over time. It may take some trial and error to find what works best for you but be patient and persistent.

Every small change brings you one step closer to becoming a more efficient and balanced CEO of the

Company of You.

Productive habits are often the ones that directly contribute to your long-term goals and personal development. These could range from daily reading for skill improvement, engaging in regular exercise to maintain physical health, to attending networking events for professional growth. These habits are characterized by their clear contribution to progress and positive outcomes in various aspects of your life. Identifying your productive habits gives you a model to assess which activities are beneficial and which ones are not.

To identify your productive habits, start by listing the activities in which you regularly engage that have a positive impact on your personal and professional life. Then, categorize them based on their impact on different areas such as health, career, relationships, or personal development. Some questions that might help in this process are:

- *What activities make you feel energized and motivated?*

- *Which ones contribute directly to achieving your goals?*

- *What habits are aligned with your personal and professional values?*

- *What activities lead to demonstrable improvement or progress in your desired areas?*

The insights gained from answering these questions will help you establish a clear understanding of what productive habits look like for you. These are habits that contribute positively to various domains of your life, align with your goals, and reflect your values.

With your productive habits identified, you can now compare them with the list of your daily activities from your journal.

This comparison will shed light on which habits are unproductive or counterproductive. Any habit that drains your energy, diverts your focus, or consumes time without providing substantial benefits can be considered unproductive.

Remember, the goal isn't to eliminate all unproductive habits. Everyone needs downtime and activities they enjoy, even if they're not particularly "productive" in the traditional sense. The objective here is to strike a balance and ensure that unproductive habits aren't hindering your progress or dominating your daily routine. Understanding and identifying your productive and unproductive habits is a powerful exercise in self-awareness. It allows you to assess where your time and energy are being spent and whether these investments align with your goals and aspirations.

Eliminating unproductive habits isn't about creating a regimented life devoid of relaxation or pleasure. It's about optimizing the way you spend your time to maximize your productivity and happiness. The key is to develop a foundational balance that allows you to achieve your goals while also enjoying your journey.

You, and only you, hold the power to shape your life, your habits, and ultimately, your success. Make the conscious choice to invest your time and energy in habits that drive you towards your goals and resonate with your values. Remember, every small change you make today will have a profound impact on your tomorrow.

Your habits are a mirror reflecting your life's direction. By understanding and refining them, you can steer your life towards your desired destination. Harness this power, transform your habits, and become the master of your own success story. Now, as the CEO, it's time to act. Make a commitment to yourself to start identifying and refining your habits today for a brighter and more fulfilling tomorrow.

Self-Care Strategies

Self-care forms the foundation of maintaining your overall well-being. In this section, we will explore various self-care strategies that encompass different aspects of your life. Practicing mindfulness, for instance, can help you remain present and cultivate a deeper understanding of your emotions and thought patterns. Engaging in physical activity is another crucial self-care strategy, as it not only enhances your physical health but also triggers the release of endorphins, contributing to improved mental well-being.

In addition, cultivating healthy eating habits, taking breaks, and setting boundaries between work and personal life are essential to ensure the maintenance of a balanced lifestyle. Prioritizing self-care activities in your daily routine is key to achieving holistic wellness and personal growth.

As we navigate the operations of the Company of You, it becomes evident that ensuring your personal well-being is the foundation upon which everything else is built. No amount of success or achievement can make up for a lack of mental & physical well-being. Therefore, it is imperative to ensure the quality of your life by adopting effective self-care strategies. Within the Quality Assurance department of The Company of You, we concentrate on the holistic wellness of the 'employee' – which is you. Just as a company cannot thrive without content and healthy employees, you cannot reach your full potential without prioritizing your well-being.

Self-care is not a luxury; it is a necessity. It guarantees that you are at your best physically, emotionally, and mentally. This encompasses, but is not limited to, maintaining a healthy lifestyle, managing stress, nurturing relationships, pursuing hobbies, and allocating time for relaxation and reflection. Recognize that self-care is a unique journey, manifesting differently for everyone.

Are you prepared to invest in your well-being? This far into the book, I imagine you are. Acknowledging the pivotal role self-care assumes in overall well-being, it's essential to understand that it's not a one-size-fits-all approach. What proves effective for one person might not necessarily yield the same results for another. Your self-care strategies ought to be tailored to your specific needs, preferences, and lifestyle. Experiment with various approaches to identify those that resonate with you and leave you feeling rejuvenated and invigorated. Remember, self-care is not synonymous with self-indulgence; rather, it's about self-preservation. It involves shaping a lifestyle that empowers you to perform optimally, both in your personal and professional spheres.

Neglecting self-care could lead to diminishing energy levels, declining productivity, and a reduced overall sense of contentment in life.

Consider the diverse dimensions of your well-being: physical, emotional, social, intellectual, and spiritual. Strive to integrate activities and practices catering to each of these dimensions into your routine. For instance: you could partake in physical exercise to enhance your physical health, engage in mindful meditation to nurture your spiritual well-being, participate in social activities to enrich your social health, and pursue continuous learning to foster intellectual growth.

In today's hyper-connected world, it can be all too easy to let work seep into your personal time. Establishing clear boundaries helps to ensure you have adequate time for relaxation and self-care.

Lastly, bear in mind that seeking assistance when needed is perfectly acceptable. Whether you're reaching out to a trusted friend or seeking professional guidance from a counselor or therapist, it remains crucial to have a support network to rely upon during challenging times.

You need not shoulder everything by yourself. After all, even the most accomplished CEOs rely on advisors and mentors for guidance. Embrace this: The path to self-actualization isn't a solitary expedition, but a shared voyage filled with enriching experiences, invaluable lessons, and heartwarming companionships.

Self-care strategies are essential for sustaining your well-being and ensuring optimal performance in the various roles you undertake as the CEO of the Company of You. Recognizing that upholding your physical, emotional, social, intellectual, and spiritual health is paramount, these strategies can foster resilience and enable you to thrive in the face of life's myriad challenges.

Nevertheless, even with the most well-honed self-care regimen, stress is an inevitable aspect of life. With mounting responsibilities and pressures, the risk of burnout becomes substantial. The subsequent section delves into a pivotal facet of your personal well-being:

Stress Management and Burnout Prevention.

As we transition to this crucial subject, keep in mind that acknowledging stress is the initial stride toward its management. Ignoring or negating its presence merely allows it to accumulate, potentially resulting in burnout.

Hence, as we progress, carry with you the significance of self-awareness and the bravery to confront and tackle challenges head-on, contributing to a balanced and gratifying existence.
Now, let's navigate the complexities of stress management and burnout prevention. It is important you possess the tools to confront the trials that arise and continue flourishing as the guide of your exceptional journey.

Unchecked stress and burnout can have significant repercussions on your physical, mental, and emotional well-being, as well as on your personal and professional relationships.

The practice of relaxation techniques, such as deep breathing exercises and progressive muscle relaxation, can be instrumental in reducing stress and tension. It is important to set realistic expectations for yourself and cultivating a robust support system involving friends, family, and colleagues can help mitigate the impact of stress and burnout.

Recognizing and addressing the signs of stress and burnout in their early stages is essential to prevent them from evolving into chronic conditions. By taking proactive measures, you can ensure that you maintain a healthy balance across all aspects of your life.

The first step in managing stress and burnout is awareness. Understanding the triggers that lead to these overwhelming states is crucial. These triggers can encompass a wide range of factors, from an excessive workload and challenging interpersonal dynamics to struggles with work-life equilibrium.

Begin by maintaining a stress journal where you can document your feelings, thoughts, and observations when you sense stress encroaching. Identifying recurring patterns in these triggers can guide you in developing personalized strategies for stress management.

Develop a growth mindset, which perceives challenges as opportunities for learning and personal development, can help reframe stress as a positive and motivating force. By shifting your perspective on stress, you can leverage it to enhance your performance and overall growth. While this mental shift may pose challenges, it is entirely achievable.

Building resilience is crucial for managing stress and preventing burnout. It's not about avoiding stress altogether, but rather about thriving in the face of adversity. This can be achieved by maintaining a positive mindset, keeping things in perspective, embracing change as a natural part of life, and fostering strong, supportive relationships.

At the core of stress and burnout management lies self-care, a fact that should not be underestimated. Just as we discussed earlier about self-care; ensuring regular physical activity, maintaining a nutritious diet, obtaining adequate sleep, and dedicating time to hobbies and interests are all fundamental components of self-care that can bolster your resilience and overall well-being.

Remember, effective stress and burnout management do not entail eliminating stress entirely, as this is both impractical and unattainable.

Instead, it involves acquiring the skills to control stress levels and prevent them from escalating into burnout. The tools and strategies discussed in this section can empower you to navigate life's inevitable stressors with greater ease, contributing to an enhanced quality of life, improved relationships, and heightened productivity.

Incorporating mindfulness practices can be instrumental in improving your capacity to manage stress and prevent burnout. Mindfulness involves anchoring your attention to the present moment and accepting it without judgment. This practice enables you to step back and observe your thoughts and emotions objectively, making it easier to recognize when stress is intensifying and intervene before it progresses to burnout. There are various avenues for practicing mindfulness, ranging from dedicated meditation sessions to integrating mindfulness into everyday activities like eating or walking.

Establishing clear boundaries between your professional and personal life is another key element in stress and burnout management. This becomes particularly pertinent in the digital era, where technology can blur these boundaries, making it challenging to disengage from work-related tasks and responsibilities. Creating designated 'work-free' zones within your home, setting specific 'offline' periods, and routinely engaging in digital detoxes are effective ways to delineate these boundaries.

The value of social connections in managing stress and preventing burnout should not be underestimated. Nurturing relationships with family, friends, and colleagues can provide a valuable support network. Sharing your experiences and emotions with others can help alleviate stress, while their unique perspectives and advice can offer fresh insights and solutions to the challenges you may face.

Keep in mind that you don't need to implement all these strategies at once. Start with one or two that resonate most with you, and gradually incorporate more as you notice improvements in your stress levels and overall well-being. Remember that this is a journey, and the key is to keep moving forward, no matter how small the steps may seem. Through proactive management and heightened awareness, you can transform stress and burnout from overwhelming adversaries into manageable aspects of your journey toward success and self-fulfillment.

7

Acknowledging Your Achievements

Congratulations on completing the Company of You program! As the CEO of your life, you've started your cultivation of a strong personal brand, set, and achieved your goals, and attained optimal health and well-being.

Throughout our exploration of various aspects of your personal and professional life, encompassing strategies for self-awareness, effective time management, optimizing your daily routine, maintaining well-being, and mitigating stress and burnout, we have now reached a pivotal moment. It's time to pause, reflect on your journey, and celebrate your accomplishments. Within the Company of You, each milestone reached, every obstacle surmounted, and every insight gained on the path to self-fulfillment deserves recognition and celebration.

Reflection is a powerful tool that enables you to learn from your past, savor your present, and shape your future. It offers perspective, insight, and comprehension, propelling personal growth and learning. As you advance towards self-actualization, it's crucial to regularly assess your experiences, review your actions, applaud your achievements, glean wisdom from setbacks, and acknowledge your personal evolution.

The purpose of this reflection isn't to pass judgment or criticize but to gain understanding and foster growth. You are your most significant investor – you've committed time, effort, and resources to your personal and professional development. Much like an annual shareholders' meeting in the corporate world, this period of reflection serves to report on the year's activities, celebrate triumphs, address challenges, and set the stage for future aspirations.

Whether this practice takes the form of daily reflections through journaling, or an annual retreat dedicated to self-reflection and goal setting, the act of looking back to propel forward can provide a refreshing sense of clarity, purpose, and direction. As we delve into the concept of 'Celebrating Your Success,' remember that it's not solely about major victories or grand milestones; it encompasses every step, every endeavor, and every moment of growth on this transformative journey.

Are you ready to step into the boardroom of self-reflection and acknowledge your achievements within the Company of You?

Let's proceed and celebrate **YOU**.

Reflecting on Your Journey

Taking time to reflect on your journey is a valuable exercise that can provide you with perspective and help you identify areas for improvement. In this section, we will delve into various methods for reflecting on your journey, including maintaining a journal, seeking feedback from others, and pausing to acknowledge your progress.

As we approach the culmination of this transformative journey through the Company of You, it's essential to take a moment to reflect on all the departments we've explored, the strategies we've employed, and the challenges we've overcome.

The Human Resources Department empowered us to recognize and nurture our unique strengths and talents, while the Marketing Department assisted us in crafting and promoting our distinctive personal brand. The Strategy Department guided us in setting ambitious yet attainable goals and provided approaches to track our progress and overcome any obstacles in our path.

We also visited the Finance Department, where we learned to understand our value, measure our accomplishments, and evaluate our personal growth. Finally, in the Operations Department, we discovered how to optimize our daily lives for efficiency and maintain a delicate balance between work and personal life, facilitating a harmonious existence.

Throughout this journey, you have not only been the CEO but also the most valuable asset of the Company of You. Your investments of time, energy, and resources in the various departments of your life will yield dividends of personal growth, success, and fulfillment.

Remember, as the CEO, your journey does not end here. Just like any successful company, the Company of You should continue to evolve, innovate, and grow.

Utilize the principles and strategies from this book to keep nurturing your talents, shaping your personal brand, setting new goals, and evaluating your progress.

Take time to celebrate your successes and learn from the setbacks.

The adventure of leading the Company of You is continuous, with each new day presenting a new opportunity to learn, grow, and succeed.

The Company of You is not merely a business entity but also a reflection of who you are and who you aspire to be. As you close this book and move forward, remember to lead your company with courage, wisdom, and integrity.

Here's to your journey of personal growth and self-fulfillment. Continue to be the extraordinary CEO of the most important company in the world—the Company of You!

Celebrating your successes, big or small, provides a well-deserved sense of accomplishment. It boosts your self-confidence and motivation, reinforcing the positive behavior that led to the achievement. Whether mastering a new skill, achieving a milestone in your personal life, or successfully implementing a self-improvement strategy, each victory deserves recognition.

Reflection is the key to fully appreciate these triumphs.

When reflecting on your journey, consider the following questions:

- *What were your most significant accomplishments this year, and why do they matter to you?*

- *What strengths and skills did you utilize to achieve these successes?*

- *What challenges did you face along the way, and how did you overcome them?*

- *What have you learned from these experiences, and how can you apply these insights moving forward?*

- *How have these achievements contributed to your overall goal of self-actualization?*

Reflecting on these questions will enable you to comprehensively evaluate your growth and progress. It will help you identify your strengths, appreciate your resilience, understand your learning, and value your journey.

Furthermore, don't limit your reflections to solo sessions. Engage with your support network—your mentors, colleagues, friends, or family—and celebrate your achievements with them. Sharing your successes not only strengthens your relationships but also broadens your perspective, offering you valuable insights that you may not have considered. Make it a normalcy within your network to regularly speak of, and support, your own and other's accomplishments.

Remember, reflection and celebration go hand in hand. As

you acknowledge your achievements, you are also celebrating the effort, perseverance, and grit that you put into realizing your goals. This balance of reflection and celebration fuels your motivation, equips you with knowledge, and strengthens your resolve to continue your journey of self-actualization.

As we navigate through this reflective journey, remember that there is no one-size-fits-all approach. It's about what works best for you, and above all, it's about appreciating the unique path you're carving out on the journey of the Company of You.

Reflection is more than just a momentary pause; it's an ongoing process that brings awareness and insight. It creates space for you to step back and evaluate your actions and decisions, their results, and the emotions and thoughts accompanying them. It is through reflection that we learn, grow, and make more informed decisions.

As you navigate your journey, it's important to develop the habit of maintaining a 'Reflection Journal.' This journal can be a dedicated space where you chronicle your thoughts, ideas, challenges, and triumphs. Regular entries can help you track your progress, observe patterns in your behavior, and identify areas of strength and growth.

In your Reflection Journal, consider recording:

Daily Achievements: What did you achieve today, however big or small? By jotting down even the smallest victories, you create a record of positivity and success to look back on and learn from during challenging times.

Challenges: What hurdles did you face today, and how did you navigate them? Reflecting on your struggles allows you to analyze your problem-solving skills and resilience.

Learnings: What lessons did you learn today? This could be from a book, conversation, or even a mistake. By recording these insights, you create a repository of wisdom.

Gratitude: What are you thankful for today? Cultivating gratitude is scientifically proven to boost happiness and resilience. This continuous self-dialogue serves to construct an accurate narrative of your journey, capturing not only the peaks and troughs but also the speed bumps and smooth highways. It offers you a comprehensive view of your growth, extending beyond mere quantitative achievements.

Consider dedicating time for reflection at the close of each day. This practice not only provides closure to your day but also aids in unwinding. Don't forget to revisit your journal entries periodically; they serve as a testament to your evolution, providing an honest account of your journey.

By nurturing a deeper relationship with yourself through reflection, you are celebrating the essence of the Company of You. The Company thrives on curiosity, resilience, ambition, and, most importantly, self-understanding and love.

You are the most important, and powerful asset, and the company's success is deeply entwined with your growth and fulfillment.

So, here's to celebrating you and your journey—the journey of a lifetime.

While maintaining a physical Reflection Journal offers

numerous benefits, it's worth acknowledging that there are alternatives. One such alternative is the mental Reflection Journal—a practice of conscious, structured mental reflection.

Like the traditional journal, a mental Reflection Journal serves as a space to chronicle your experiences, insights, and growth. However, it operates within the confines of your mind. This method of journaling is more fluid, less time-bound, and can be practiced at any time. **Mental journaling involves honing your mindfulness and introspection skills. Here's a suggested process to get started:**

1. **Mindful Moments:** Dedicate quiet moments throughout your day to pause and reflect. These moments could occur during your morning coffee, a mid-day walk, or even a late-night stargazing session. Choose moments that align with your schedule and preferences.

2. **Focused Reflection:** During these mindful moments, engage in conscious reflection on the same themes as your physical journal—your accomplishments, challenges, lessons learned, and moments of gratitude. Immerse yourself in the detailed recollection of your experiences, fully engaging your senses and emotions.

3. **Mental Bookmarking:** As you sift through the day's experiences, mentally bookmark the significant ones. Visualization can be a powerful tool for this step. For example, imagine placing a specific achievement or newfound insight into a mental "treasure chest" or "library."

4. **Revisit & Recall:** Make it a routine to revisit your

mental bookmarks regularly. Like a physical journal, the potency of this practice lies in revisiting and connecting the dots between your experiences.

5.   **Verbal Sharing:** Sharing your reflections with someone else can solidify your mental notes. Whether it's a loved one, a mentor, or a reflection partner, verbalizing your thoughts and insights creates an auditory record of your reflections, enhancing your ability to recall and learn.

While a mental Reflection Journal may not leave behind a physical record, the imprints it leaves within your mind can be profoundly impactful. This practice fosters mental agility, bolsters memory retention, and cultivates heightened self-awareness. Consistency and deliberate reflection are the keys to its effectiveness. The beauty of the Reflection Journal, whether physical or mental, lies in its ability to reflect the uniqueness of your journey.

There is no universal template; it's your personal narrative, narrated in your distinctive voice. As you progress along your path, embracing the art of reflection empowers you to understand your journey more profoundly. This allows you to celebrate your growth and accomplishments the right way.

The potency of reflection, whether through a physical journal or mental notations, cannot be overstated. It furnishes us with profound insights into our journey, enabling us to recognize our growth, celebrate our achievements, and learn from our experiences. As we peruse the pages of our past, we enrich our present and mold our future with greater awareness and intentionality.

Introspection naturally leads us to the profound practice of gratitude. Gratitude empowers us to acknowledge the worth in our lives, transforming our perception of ordinary moments into extraordinary ones.

In the next section, "Embracing Gratitude," we will touch on the transformative power of gratitude and its integral role in recognizing our accomplishments, enhancing our well-being, and guiding us toward a fulfilling future. So, as we set down our Reflection Journal, let us open our hearts to a new chapter of gratitude.

Cultivating Gratitude

Cultivating gratitude is a powerful approach to nurturing a positive mindset and maintaining unwavering motivation. In this section, we'll delve into the many advantages of gratitude, including increased resilience, improved relationships, and enhanced overall well-being.

We'll also explore practical ways to incorporate gratitude into your daily life, such as maintaining a gratitude journal, expressing appreciation to those around you, and focusing on the positive aspects of your life.

The practice of gratitude has a well-established track record for positively affecting our mental, emotional, and physical well-being. By consistently directing our attention towards the positive aspects of life, we train our minds to seek out and amplify the good, resulting in a more optimistic and positive outlook. This shift towards positivity can fortify our ability to bounce back from challenges, enrich our relationships, and contribute to an overarching sense of contentment and satisfaction in life.

Embracing gratitude isn't just about recognizing the positives in your life; it involves allowing that recognition to influence your perspective on life, your interactions with others, and your self-perception. As the CEO of the Company of You, fostering an attitude of gratitude can provide a solid foundation for a positive, resilient, and fulfilling life. Gratitude, often overshadowed in our fast-paced lives, possesses the power to transform our personal and professional journey. It's not merely about saying 'thank you.' Instead, it encourages us to shift our focus, appreciate the present moment, and cultivate positive relationships.

Let's begin with resilience, a crucial quality for navigating life's challenges. We've all faced obstacles, setbacks, and failures along the way. While these experiences are undoubtedly challenging, they also offer opportunities for growth and learning. Through the lens of gratitude, these hurdles can be seen as valuable life lessons. Expressing gratitude for these experiences allows us to acknowledge our inner strength, resilience, and ability to adapt and grow.

Shifting our focus to relationships, gratitude acts as a bridge, nurturing deeper connections. Simple gestures like appreciating others with a 'thank you' or a heartfelt note of acknowledgment are expressions of gratitude. They convey our understanding and appreciation of the efforts or qualities of the other person. Consequently, this strengthens our bond with them, making our relationships deeper, more satisfying, and enriching.

Gratitude is more than just an emotion; it's an action, a practice that needs to be integrated into our daily lives. One effective method is maintaining a gratitude journal. Scientifically proven to enhance well-being and satisfaction, the act of writing down things we're grateful for compels us to pause and reflect on the positives, even on challenging days. A physical journal isn't a requirement; digital notes or simply mental acknowledgments work just as effectively. What matters is the process of consciously recognizing and acknowledging the positives in our lives.

Moreover, the practice of gratitude offers an array of mental health benefits. It counters negative emotions, reducing feelings of envy, resentment, and frustration. It fosters happiness, reducing depression and boosting mental resilience.

By merely acknowledging the good, we're training our minds to focus on the positive aspects, cultivating a positive mindset.

Integrating gratitude into our routines is like installing a lens of positivity. Through it, we learn to savor joyful moments, derive lessons from challenging experiences, and cherish the relationships we cultivate. This practice directs our attention to our past achievements and illuminates the path toward future successes. It's not a one-time act but a continual process—a journey of acknowledging our blessings and cherishing our progress.

Now, let's explore how to utilize gratitude in a professional context. Gratitude in the workplace correlates with increased job satisfaction, productivity, and team morale, while reducing stress and burnout. Cultivating a culture of appreciation fosters an environment promoting mutual respect, collaboration, and job satisfaction.

Gratitude at work can manifest in various forms—a note of appreciation to a colleague, acknowledgment of a job well done, or recognizing the team's efforts in a project. It also means expressing thanks for opportunities to learn and grow, stemming from both successes and failures. When challenges are viewed as chances for growth and gratitude is expressed for these learning experiences, a more resilient and positive work culture is shaped.

Essentially, gratitude serves as a transformative tool across life's journey, whether fostering personal resilience, enriching relationships, or nurturing a positive work culture.

Now, within the framework of 'The Company of You,' let's delve into how gratitude can be harnessed as a transformative tool to thrive in this ever-changing world. Much like investing in a valuable business, it's about investing in yourself, fostering growth, development, and self-actualization.

As the CEO of 'The Company of You,' you are the primary stakeholder and the most asset. Acknowledging and appreciating your efforts, celebrating victories, and appreciating progress are equally crucial, just as a company acknowledges its employees to enhance morale and productivity.

Gratitude plays a pivotal role in your personal growth journey. It paves the way for self-actualization—the realization and fulfillment of your potential. Expressing gratitude for your unique abilities, talents, and strengths reaffirms your value, boosts self-esteem, and enhances self-confidence. It encourages you to focus on your unique qualities, nurturing a positive self-image that propels you to pursue goals and aspirations with renewed vigor.

Similarly, acknowledging challenges and expressing gratitude for them leads to personal growth. Challenges offer opportunities to learn, adapt, and cultivate resilience. Each challenge invites growth beyond your comfort zone. Viewing them through a lens of gratitude transforms them into valuable lessons, steppingstones on the path to self-actualization.

Gratitude also establishes the foundation for continuous improvement, a pivotal aspect of 'The Company of You' growth strategy. Being grateful for feedback and constructive criticism nurtures a growth mindset, considering every piece of advice as a chance to learn and refine skills.

Gratitude strengthens relationships by fostering a spirit of generosity and reciprocity. Expressing gratitude toward those in your life validates their efforts and cultivates stronger, more meaningful relationships. These are the relationships that create a robust support network, a vital asset, as we discussed, for 'The Company of You.'

Integrating gratitude into your life and 'The Company of You' goes beyond mere expressions of 'thank you.' It involves cultivating an attitude of appreciation, perceiving the world in a way that emphasizes positives, identifies opportunities in challenges, and treasures the journey as much as the destination. Embracing this attitude nurtures a positive mindset, fosters resilience, and opens the path to self-actualization.

Take away from this section: gratitude isn't just a tool but a way of life. It's an essential ingredient for self-growth and self-actualization, a catalyst capable of transforming 'The Company of You' into a thriving enterprise—one that perseveres amid challenges and flourishes amid success.

Let's continue this journey, fostering gratitude, treasuring progress, and moving closer to self-actualization.

Planning for Your Future

As we approach the culmination of our transformative journey, it's time to shift our focus toward the future and fully embrace the power of Continuous Improvement.

Continuous Improvement, a principle that lies at the heart of both personal and professional growth, entails the unwavering commitment to making incremental enhancements over time. As we advance along our journey toward self-actualization, we should embrace this philosophy as a cornerstone of our long-term growth strategy.

The concept behind Continuous Improvement is elegantly simple: instead of striving for monumental, instantaneous changes, concentrate on implementing small, manageable improvements consistently. Over time, these modest adjustments accumulate, resulting in substantial growth and development. By adopting this mindset, we can cultivate a culture of perpetual learning and improvement within 'The Company of You.'

Remember, 'The Company of You' is not a static destination; it's an ever-evolving journey, a continual process of growth and development.

Continuous Improvement signifies your unwavering commitment to this journey, your unceasing aspiration to become better, and your dedication to shaping a future where you continually unlock your boundless potential. Whether it's honing a specific skill, bolstering your physical well-being, or fortifying emotional resilience, every facet of your life can reap the rewards of the Continuous Improvement principle.

The objective here is not unattainable perfection; it's the constant pursuit of progress. It's about relentlessly advancing, regardless of how incremental each step may seem. By diligently celebrating your successes, thoughtfully reflecting on your journey, wholeheartedly embracing gratitude, and meticulously planning for your future, you can continue to evolve and thrive in your role as the CEO of your life. Always remember that the Company of You is an unceasing journey, and the key to long-term success and profound fulfillment lies in the steadfast commitment to continuous improvement.

A Legacy

Leaving a legacy is an inherent part of our human longing to make a meaningful imprint on the world. It symbolizes the culmination of our personal and professional growth — a testimony to the positive transformations we have instigated in the lives of others and the indelible mark we are engraving upon the annals of time.

At the heart of leaving a legacy lies the pivotal act of aligning our actions with our core values and passions. Our values embody what holds the utmost significance for us — they are the guiding principles that mold our decisions and steer our behaviors. By fully comprehending and wholeheartedly embracing our core values, we can ensure that our actions resonate harmoniously with our beliefs, thus bequeathing an authentic and heartfelt legacy that mirrors our true selves.

Equally indispensable is the identification of our passions. What sets our souls ablaze and stirs the depths of our hearts? What causes, issues, or pursuits strike a profound chord within us? It is when we tap into our passions that we draw from an unending wellspring of purpose and fulfillment. Through our passions, we gain the power to forge a profound and enduring impact, for it is when we are genuinely impassioned about something that we invest our time, energy, and resources with unwavering dedication.

Once our core values and passions are unveiled, we are

poised to explore the avenues for effecting positive change. The act of making a difference in the lives of others and in the broader world can manifest itself in myriad ways. It may materialize through acts of kindness and compassion, the simple extension of a helping hand to those in need. It might take shape as mentorship and guidance, the empowerment of others to unlock their full potential. It could also emerge as innovative ideas and solutions, addressing the challenges facing society and propelling the wheels of positive transformation. By harnessing our skills, resources, and sphere of influence, we wield the capability to initiate a far-reaching ripple effect of positive impact that extends well beyond the boundaries of our immediate circle of influence.

Crafting a deliberate legacy plan represents the ultimate step in ensuring the enduring impact of our journey. A legacy plan serves as a blueprint, outlining our vision, goals, and actionable steps required to manifest the legacy we aspire to leave. It involves setting clear intentions and identifying specific ways in which we can contribute to the greater good.

A well-crafted legacy plan provides us with a roadmap, guiding our decisions and actions, and helping us remain steadfastly focused on what genuinely matters. It serves as a compass, ensuring that every step we take aligns harmoniously with our purpose and actively contributes to the legacy we envision.

As we conclude this transformative voyage within "The Company of You," let us wholeheartedly embrace the idea that our legacy extends beyond personal success; it encompasses the positive change we instigate in the world. By leaving a legacy, we ensure that our impact continues to resonate long after our time on this Earth, leaving an indelible mark that inspires and uplifts future generations.

It's vital to remember that the magnitude of your achievements or the accolades you receive does not define your legacy. Rather, it's determined by the lives you touch, the difference you make, and the lasting impression you leave on the hearts of others.

Embrace the opportunity to leave a profound and enduring legacy, guided by your core values and passions, and driven by the desire to create positive change. Your legacy reflects the incredible person you have become, and it will continue to inspire and empower others long after your journey.

"The Company of You" transcends mere metaphorical meaning; it embodies the extraordinary potential within each of us to design a life rich in purpose, passion, and fulfillment.

As the CEO of this remarkable organization, you hold the key to unlocking your true potential and evolving into the finest version of yourself. You've embarked on a journey of self-discovery, growth, and empowerment, acknowledging the significance of lifelong learning and advancement.

Throughout the diverse concepts and theory, you've explored, accumulating insights, strategies, and tools to navigate the complexities of life, surmount challenges, and seize personal and professional success opportunities. You've cultivated a growth mindset, harnessed your unique strengths and talents, developed a compelling personal brand, and recognized the significance of balance, resilience, and self-care.

"The Company of You" is not merely a book; it serves as a blueprint for leading a life infused with purpose and fulfillment. It stands as a reminder that you are the architect of your destiny, the conductor of your symphony, and the master of your journey. It proves that you possess the power to effect change, to craft a legacy that resonates deeply with those you influence.

As you conclude this experience, carry forward the lessons, insights, and wisdom you've gained. Embrace gratitude, continuous improvement, and the pursuit of leaving a positive impact as lifelong companions. Reflect on your journey, celebrate your achievements, and remember that growth and success are perpetual processes. In the grand symphony of life, your role as the CEO of "The Company of You" is ever evolving. It entails a continuous commitment to personal and professional growth, a dedication to making a positive impact, and an unwavering journey of self-actualization.

Therefore, step forward with confidence, passion, and a profound sense of purpose. Embrace the adventure that lies ahead and allow the Company of You to serve as the bedrock upon which you construct a life of remarkable success, happiness, and fulfillment.

Congratulations on successfully completing this extraordinary journey within "The Company of You."

The best is yet to come!

A Personal Invitation from the Author

As we reach the conclusion of "The Company of You," I, Zachary Italian, extend a heartfelt invitation to you to continue this transformative journey. Your path to self-actualization and professional success does not end with the last page of this book. It's just the beginning.

Join The More Core

Visit:

https://core.youdeservemore.media

In the "More Core" community, you will discover a world of opportunities to connect, grow, and thrive. This community embodies the spirit of the lessons and principles we've explored together in the book.

What You'll Find at More Core?

- Dynamic Networking Opportunities: Connect with professionals and entrepreneurs who are just as passionate and driven as you are.

- Exclusive Learning Materials: Gain access to a rich repository of resources, including webinars, e-books, and insightful articles focused on personal and professional development.

- Guidance from Experts: Receive personalized advice and mentorship from seasoned professionals and industry leaders.

- Inspirational Events: Participate in workshops and seminars designed to motivate and educate, pushing you further on your path to success.

I would love to hear from you and learn about your journey. You can reach out to me directly at:

- Email: zach@youdeservemore.media

Let's continue to build and grow together.

Your story is just beginning, and I can't wait to see where it leads.